A Compassionate Guide to Parenting a child with
AUTISM

Every Insight an Inquisitive Parent Needs to Empower, Understand, and Thrive

DR. MURCHANA KHOUND

INDIA • SINGAPORE • MALAYSIA

ISBN
Paperback 979-8-89632-778-3
Hardcase 979-8-89673-733-9

Preface

Understanding autism isn't just about medical definitions or checklists—it's about stepping into a world full of unique perspectives, special challenges, and incredible strengths. This book is here to guide parents, caregivers, and anyone looking to understand Autism Spectrum Disorder (ASD) in a simple and compassionate way. It is meant to offer both knowledge and hope, helping families turn uncertainty into confidence and challenges into opportunities.

Every chapter has been carefully written to address the many questions and concerns that come up when a family starts to navigate autism. It explains the condition in clear terms, offers practical advice, and gives parents the tools to create an environment where their child can thrive. Through these pages, we hope to replace fear with understanding and inspire confidence in the incredible potential of every child.

The book is filled with stories—some based on real experiences, others crafted to help explain ideas better. These stories will take you into the lives of children and parents, like Aarav, whose love for toy cars helped his family understand his sensory needs. These examples make autism easier to understand, while protecting the privacy of real families.

Inside, you'll learn about:

- **What Autism Is**: A simple and compassionate explanation of ASD, including early signs and the journey to diagnosis. Aarav's story brings these ideas to life.

- **Autism Around the World**: How awareness has grown globally and in India, breaking barriers and giving families better access to support.

- **Facts and Myths**: Clear up common misconceptions about autism so you can feel confident and informed as a parent.

- **Signs Across Ages**: Autism looks different at every age. Learn how to recognize and respond to your child's unique developmental needs.

- **Autism Traits**: A closer look at key characteristics, like social challenges and repetitive behaviors, explained through relatable examples.

- **Other Conditions**: Autism often comes with other challenges, like sensory sensitivities or medical conditions. Find practical strategies for addressing them.

- **First Steps**: What to do when autism becomes a question in your life—how to seek help, find the right therapies, and build a support system.

This book combines research, real-life stories, and actionable advice to make your journey smoother. It aims to connect knowledge with empathy, giving families the strength to face challenges and celebrate progress.

Our Goal

This book is more than information—it's a source of hope and encouragement. Autism is not a barrier but a spectrum of unique strengths waiting to be nurtured. We want every parent and caregiver to feel supported and empowered as they help their child grow and shine.

As you read, we hope these pages bring you inspiration, comfort, and a sense of purpose. This journey is one of discovery, love, and endless possibilities. Welcome to it!

Dr. Murchana Khound

Foreword

Autism Spectrum Disorder (ASD) is a subject that demands not just academic rigor but also profound empathy and understanding. In this transformative book, Dr. Murchana Khound brings both to the table, creating a work that is as insightful as it is compassionate. Drawing on her years of clinical experience in Pediatrics, Neonatology, and Developmental Neurology, she has crafted a guide that not only informs but also empowers parents, caregivers, and educators to better understand and support children on the autism spectrum.

As the Executive Director of AIIMS Guwahati, I have witnessed firsthand the critical importance of awareness and early intervention in improving the lives of children with autism and their families. This book resonates deeply with that mission. Dr. Khound's approach to explaining the nuances of autism—whether discussing early signs, co-occurring conditions, or the myths that cloud understanding—is both accessible and enlightening. The use of heartfelt stories woven into evidence-based practices adds a dimension of relatability that makes this book a true companion for families navigating the journey of autism.

What makes this book unique is its holistic vision. It delves into therapies, dietary insights, and the celebration of neurodiversity, underscoring Dr. Khound's commitment to fostering a world where every child can thrive. Her message is clear: autism is not a limitation but a spectrum of extraordinary abilities waiting to be nurtured.

This book is a beacon of hope and knowledge. I am confident it will inspire parents, caregivers, and professionals alike to reimagine their approach to autism and build a brighter, more inclusive future.

Dr (Prof.) Ashok Puranik
Executive Director, AIIMS Guwahati

Contents

Chapter 1

What is Autism?
A Simple Overview for Parents

A Story of Discovery: Meet Aarav

When Aarav was three years old, his parents began to notice some differences in his behavior. While other children his age were eagerly calling out "Mama" or "Papa," Aarav didn't say much at all. Instead, he was fascinated by spinning the wheels of his toy car, watching them turn for hours. At the playground, Aarav didn't seem interested in joining the other children. He preferred to sit in a quiet corner, lining up his toy cars in perfect rows. His mother, Priya, worried when he didn't respond to his name or make eye contact, but well-meaning friends and relatives assured her, "He's just shy—he'll grow out of it."

Priya and her husband, Raj, decided to trust their instincts. They scheduled a visit to their pediatrician, who referred them to a developmental specialist. After several observations and evaluations, Aarav was diagnosed with Autism Spectrum Disorder (ASD). Though overwhelmed at first, Priya and Raj began to learn about autism. They discovered that Aarav's behaviors, like avoiding eye contact and his fascination with patterns, were part of a condition that affected how he experienced and interacted with the world. Armed with knowledge and support, they began to understand Aarav's unique strengths and challenges. Together, they started the journey of supporting him to thrive.

What is Autism?

Autism Spectrum Disorder (ASD) is a condition that affects how a child understands and interacts with the world around them. It is called a "spectrum" because children with autism have a wide range of abilities and challenges. Some may need significant support in their daily lives, while others can be highly independent but still struggle in specific areas like social interactions or managing sensory sensitivities.

Understanding autism is the first step in creating an environment where children like Aarav can flourish. Let's explore the key areas that define autism, as outlined by medical guidelines such as the DSM-5 (Diagnostic and Statistical Manual of Mental Disorders, 5th Edition).

Autism is primarily defined by two main areas of difficulty:

1. Social Communication and Interaction

Children with autism often face challenges in understanding social cues and forming connections with others. This doesn't mean they don't want relationships or friendships—it simply means they experience the world differently. Here's what these challenges can look like:

- **Difficulty forming relationships**:

    - Children with autism may prefer to play alone rather than join a group of peers. Aarav, for instance, often sat by himself at the playground, observing others but not engaging.

    - They may find it challenging to make friends, as they may not understand the give-and-take of social interactions.

- **Struggles with emotions**:

    - Recognizing emotions in others—like understanding when someone is sad or angry—can be difficult for children with autism.

    - They may also express emotions in ways you don't expect. For example, Aarav rarely smiled when someone smiled at him, but he would laugh heartily at spinning wheels.

- **Challenges with communication**:

  - Making eye contact or using gestures like pointing or waving might not come naturally.

  - Conversations can also be hard, as children with autism may not understand how to take turns speaking or might focus only on topics that interest them, like dinosaurs or trains.

2. Restricted and Repetitive Behaviors

Children with autism often find comfort in routines and repetition. They might engage in behaviors or develop interests that seem unusual to others but are a source of joy or regulation for them.

- **Repetitive movements or speech**:

  - Some children flap their hands when excited, spin in circles when overwhelmed, or repeat the same word or phrase, like Aarav's "spin, spin, spin" when he played with his toy cars.

- Adherence to Routines in Autism:

  - For many children with autism, routines are vital for comfort and stability in a chaotic world. Predictability reduces anxiety, giving them control over their environment. Aarav, for example, relied on a specific morning routine of cereal, cartoons, and lining up toy cars. When his cereal ran out one day, he became upset, unable to adapt. Realizing the importance of routines, his parents prepared backup options to maintain predictability, helping Aarav transition smoothly and feel secure.

- **Strong focus on specific interests**:

  - Many children with autism develop intense interests in specific topics, like numbers, planets, or vehicles. Aarav, for instance, could name every car brand but struggled to respond when someone asked his favorite color.

- **Sensitivity to sensory input**:

  - Loud noises, bright lights, or certain textures can overwhelm children with autism. For example, Aarav would cover his ears when the vacuum cleaner was on or refuse to wear woolen clothes because they felt "itchy." On the other hand, some children may seek sensory input, like enjoying firm hugs or touching different textures repeatedly.

Why Understanding Autism Matters

Understanding autism and recognizing its signs can profoundly impact a child's life and the journey of their family. Like Priya and Raj, who discovered a new perspective by seeing the world through Aarav's eyes, parents and caregivers can embrace their child's unique qualities and help them flourish by offering the right support and acceptance.

This book aims to serve as a trusted companion on that path. Each chapter is crafted to guide you through the early signs of autism, explain therapeutic approaches, and celebrate the strengths that make every child exceptional. Autism is not a limitation; it represents a unique way of experiencing and interacting with the world, bringing both challenges and extraordinary potential.

Every child with autism is one-of-a-kind. While some may struggle with speech but excel in logical reasoning, others might find comfort in routines while demonstrating remarkable creativity. By understanding and appreciating these differences, you can provide tailored support that nurtures your child's strengths and addresses their challenges.

With patience, awareness, and early intervention, children with autism can develop the skills to learn, grow, and thrive on their own terms. Recognizing their individuality and celebrating their potential is the key to helping them reach their full capabilities.

When Do Symptoms Appear?

Autism often reveals its signs early, with many parents noticing differences by the time their child is around 2 years old—or even sooner. However, for some children, symptoms only become apparent as social expectations increase, such as in preschool or when interacting with peers.

Imagine a one-year-old named Aarav. When his parents called his name, he wouldn't respond, often absorbed in watching the spinning wheels of his toy car. By 18 months, when other toddlers were saying "Mama" or "Ball," Aarav hadn't spoken any meaningful words. At playdates, he didn't seem interested in playing with other kids and preferred lining up his toys in perfect rows.

These are some early signs parents might notice, including:

- **No response to their name by 12 months**: While other children might turn their heads or look at you, a child with autism may seem lost in their own world.

- **No meaningful words by 18 months**: Instead of saying simple words like "milk" or "car," the child may rely on gestures or remain silent.

- **Difficulty engaging with others or toys**: The child might not know how to play with toys as intended, such as pretending to feed a doll, and may instead focus on repetitive actions, like stacking blocks endlessly.

These subtle signs can feel puzzling, but noticing them early is the first step toward understanding and supporting your child's unique developmental needs.

Chapter 2

Autism Prevalence: A Perspective from India and Around the World

A Mother's Journey: The Hidden Puzzle Pieces

When Priya's three-year-old son, Aarav, began avoiding eye contact and preferred spinning wheels over playing with other children, she brushed it off as a phase. "He's just shy," her relatives assured her, attributing his quiet demeanor to his personality. But as time passed, Priya noticed more: his sensitivity to loud sounds, his meltdowns over minor changes in routine, and his silence in social settings. Unsure and overwhelmed, Priya sought help.

Her journey led her to a pediatrician who mentioned Autism Spectrum Disorder (ASD). It was a word Priya had only heard vaguely but never fully understood. As the doctor explained, Aarav's behaviors began to make sense. The diagnosis, while initially daunting, opened doors to therapies and support that helped Aarav thrive.

Priya's story is one of countless families in India and across the globe navigating the unknown waters of autism. For many parents, understanding autism prevalence provides not just clarity but a sense of belonging in a community facing similar challenges. The increasing awareness and resources available today are creating opportunities for children like Aarav to shine in their unique ways. This chapter delves into the numbers, progress, and hope surrounding autism prevalence in India and around the world.

Autism Knows No Boundaries: A Global Perspective

Autism Spectrum Disorder (ASD) touches the lives of children and families in every corner of the world. Its presence transcends borders, cultures, and languages, uniting millions in the shared journey of understanding and acceptance. In India, where data collection has historically been a challenge, it's estimated that about 1 in 68 children are affected by autism. Globally, the numbers are similar, with 1 in 100 children identified on the spectrum. Interestingly, boys are diagnosed nearly three times as often as girls, a pattern observed universally.

Autism in India: A Story of Growing Awareness

Two decades ago, the word "autism" was barely a whisper in most Indian households. Children showing signs of the condition were often misunderstood. Parents might hear phrases like "They'll grow out of it," or "It's just a phase." Misdiagnoses were common, with autism mistaken for other behavioral or developmental issues. Families struggled without access to specialized therapies or informed professionals.

Fast forward to today, and the landscape is transforming dramatically:

- **Improved Diagnosis:** The introduction of global standards like the DSM-5 and India-specific tools like INDT-ASD has equipped healthcare providers with reliable methods to identify autism. This means fewer children are slipping through the cracks.

- **Early Screening Revolution:** Programs advocating tools like the M-CHAT-R/F and TABC are making it easier to detect autism in its earliest stages—even in remote villages. These tools are empowering parents and doctors to act swiftly.

- **The Power of Awareness:** Social media campaigns, parent support groups, and dedicated organizations are spreading awareness far and wide. Parents are recognizing the signs earlier and seeking help sooner, breaking decades of silence and stigma.

This collective effort has led to a sharp rise in diagnosed cases. It's not that autism is becoming more prevalent; it's that we're finally recognizing and naming it. Yet, challenges persist, especially in rural and underserved regions where access to trained professionals and resources remains limited. Despite this, the progress over the last 20 years has been nothing short of remarkable, offering hope to countless families across the country.

With continued awareness, collaboration, and compassion, the journey toward acceptance and support for children with autism in India is moving forward, one step at a time.

Autism Around the World: A Shared Journey

Autism Spectrum Disorder (ASD) connects millions of children and families across the globe in a shared experience of discovery, challenge, and growth. Globally, autism is estimated to affect 1 in 100 children, yet in countries like the United States, where diagnostic systems are more established, the prevalence is recorded as high as 1 in 36 children. This variation isn't due to a difference in autism itself but rather in how it is identified and reported.

Why Do Prevalence Rates Vary?

- **Diagnostic Practices:** In countries with robust healthcare systems, early screening and access to specialists mean autism is diagnosed more frequently and accurately. For instance, a well-established pediatric network in the U.S. makes it easier for parents to seek timely assessments.

- **Awareness:** Where autism awareness is high, parents, teachers, and caregivers are more likely to recognize early signs, such as delayed speech or social challenges, leading to earlier intervention and reporting.

- **Cultural Differences:** In some regions, stigma or lack of education about autism may lead to underreporting. Conversely, areas with strong surveillance systems might overreport cases due to rigorous screening.

Global Efforts for Awareness and Support

Organizations like **Autism Speaks**, the **World Health Organization (WHO)**, and countless local advocacy groups work tirelessly to educate communities, promote acceptance, and ensure families have access to necessary resources. From early intervention programs to support networks, their efforts continue to break down barriers worldwide.

Autism Prevelance – as reported by CDC – ADDM Report 2000 - 2018

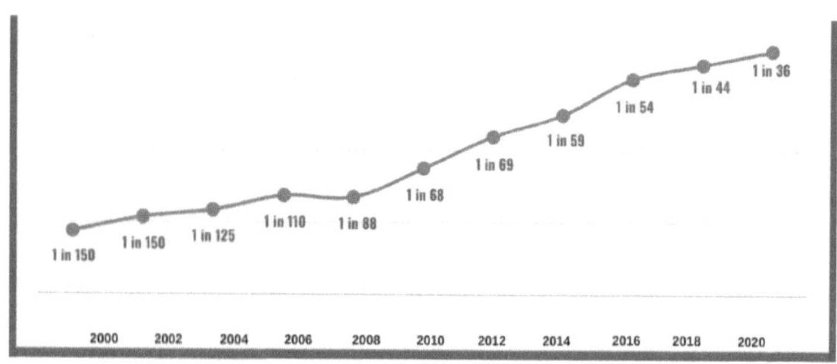

What Do These Numbers Mean for Parents?

For families navigating autism, statistics offer more than just numbers—they serve as a reminder of shared experiences and growing support systems:

- **You Are Not Alone:** Millions of parents worldwide are on the same path, creating a community where experiences are shared and understood.

- **Awareness Drives Action:** Recognizing autism early empowers families to act, providing their child with a better chance to thrive.

- **Hope is Rising:** With improved therapies, tools, and understanding, the future for children with autism is brighter than ever.

By staying informed and seeking support, parents can become advocates, paving the way for their child to navigate the world with confidence and strength. Autism isn't a limitation—it's a unique way of experiencing and contributing to the world, waiting to be understood, supported, and celebrated.

Chapter 3

Understanding the Risk Factors for Autism: Myths, Blame, and Facts

A Common Scenario

Priya had always been cautious during her pregnancy. She followed her doctor's advice, avoided junk food, and even switched to organic vegetables. When her son Aarav was diagnosed with Autism Spectrum Disorder (ASD) at age three, she was devastated. As the news spread through the family, so did the whispers.

"Maybe it's because she worked too much during pregnancy," someone speculated.

"It could be because she let Aarav watch cartoons all day," another added.

The blame game began, and Priya found herself questioning everything she had done—or hadn't done. Did she take the right vitamins? Could it be her age? Was it her fault?

Like many parents, Priya was overwhelmed with guilt and confusion. However, understanding autism's risk factors and separating myths from facts is critical for parents to move forward with clarity and confidence.

What Are the Risk Factors for Autism?

Understanding the risk factors for Autism Spectrum Disorder (ASD) is like piecing together a complex puzzle. There isn't a single cause of autism; rather, it arises from a combination of genetic, biological, and environmental influences. As parents, you might wonder: *"Did something I do contribute to this?"* The answer is reassuring—autism is not anyone's fault. Let's delve into the factors that researchers believe may increase the likelihood of autism, in a way that provides clarity and peace of mind.

1. Genetic Factors: A Family Connection

Genetics play a significant role in autism, often acting as a foundation upon which other factors build.

- **Family History**: If a sibling or close relative has been diagnosed with autism, the chances of another child in the family developing autism are higher. This familial connection suggests a strong genetic influence.

- **Gene Mutations**: Autism isn't always inherited. Sometimes, genetic mutations can occur spontaneously, during the early stages of a baby's development. These irregularities may alter how the brain grows and functions, potentially leading to autism traits.

- **Syndromic Disorders**: Certain genetic conditions, like **Fragile X Syndrome**, **Rett Syndrome**, or **tuberous sclerosis**, are often associated with autism. These conditions are rare but highlight the intricate relationship between genes and development.

What This Means for Parents: Genetics is just one piece of the puzzle. If autism runs in your family, early screening and intervention are the best steps you can take.

2. Advanced Parental Age: Does Age Matter?

The age of parents at the time of conception can also influence autism risk.

- **Older Parents**: The likelihood of autism slightly increases when mothers and fathers are older, especially beyond their late 30s or 40s. This may be due to an increased chance of genetic mutations as parents age.

- **Reproductive Health**: Conditions like infertility or the use of assisted reproductive technologies, such as IVF, have also been linked to a marginally higher autism risk, though the connection isn't fully understood.

What This Means: While parental age may play a role, it is one of many factors, and older parents can still have healthy, thriving children.

3. Prenatal and Birth-Related Factors: A Critical Window

A child's development in the womb and during birth is a critical period, and certain conditions during this time may contribute to autism.

- **Maternal Health During Pregnancy**:
  - Infections such as **rubella** or **influenza** during pregnancy have been linked to an increased risk of autism.
  - Chronic conditions like **diabetes** or **obesity** in the mother may also affect fetal brain development.

- **Birth Complications**:
  - Babies born prematurely or with low birth weight are at greater risk for developmental challenges, including autism.
  - **Oxygen deprivation** during delivery (known as hypoxia) is another significant risk factor, as it may affect the baby's brain.

- **Exposure to Certain Medications**:

  - Some medications taken during pregnancy, such as **sodium valproate** (used to treat epilepsy), have been linked to a higher likelihood of autism in the child.

What This Means: Good prenatal care and open communication with your healthcare provider can help reduce some of these risks.

4. Environmental Factors: The Role of External Influences

The environment in which a baby develops, both inside and outside the womb, can have subtle effects on brain growth.

- **Toxins**: Exposure to harmful substances like pesticides, heavy metals (e.g., lead), or air pollutants during pregnancy may impact brain development.

- **Lifestyle Factors**:

  - Smoking, alcohol consumption, or substance use during pregnancy can interfere with fetal brain growth and increase autism risk.

What This Means: Reducing exposure to harmful substances during pregnancy benefits overall health, even if it doesn't entirely eliminate autism risk.

5. Neurological Factors: Brain Development Differences

Autism is closely tied to how the brain develops during infancy and early childhood.

- **Abnormal Brain Growth**: Some children with autism experience unusually rapid brain growth during infancy.

This may result in a larger-than-average head size (macrocephaly) or differences in brain connectivity.

- **Neurotransmitter Imbalances**: The brain relies on chemicals like serotonin and dopamine for communication. Disruptions in these chemicals can influence traits associated with autism, such as sensory sensitivities or repetitive behaviors.

What This Means: Neurological differences don't define a child's potential but highlight the need for tailored support to help them thrive.

6. Gender: Why Boys Are at Higher Risk

Autism is approximately three to four times more common in boys than in girls. Researchers believe this may be due to genetic and biological differences, though the exact reasons remain unclear.

- Boys may be more susceptible to genetic mutations or have fewer protective factors in their genetic makeup.

- Girls with autism may also be underdiagnosed because they often display subtler traits or mask their symptoms better.

What This Means: Understanding these differences helps ensure that all children, regardless of gender, receive timely evaluation and support.

7. Immune System Irregularities: A Mother's Health Matters

The mother's immune system plays a vital role during pregnancy, and certain irregularities may influence autism risk.

- **Maternal Immune Activation**: If the mother's immune system is overactive due to infections or other factors during pregnancy, it can affect the developing baby's brain.

- **Autoimmune Conditions**: Mothers with autoimmune diseases like **lupus** or **rheumatoid arthritis** are slightly more likely to have children with autism.

What This Means: Managing maternal health conditions during pregnancy is essential for overall well-being, though these risks remain small.

8. Siblings with Autism: A Family Connection

Imagine you've just navigated the complexities of raising a child with autism, and then the question arises: *"What if my next child is also diagnosed?"* This concern is common and grounded in evidence.

- **Recurrence Risk**: If a family has one child with autism, the chances of another child being diagnosed increase to about **10–20%**, compared to the general population.

- The risk climbs even higher if two or more siblings have already been diagnosed.

What This Means: If you have one child with autism, early monitoring and screening for subsequent children are critical. However, remember that even if a diagnosis occurs, your experience and resources will help you navigate this journey more confidently.

9. Cultural and Diagnostic Factors: Autism Through Different Lenses

Autism doesn't discriminate—it affects children across all cultures and demographics. However, how autism is recognized and diagnosed can vary significantly based on societal awareness and resources.

- **Underdiagnosis or Misdiagnosis**: In regions where autism awareness is limited, behaviors associated with ASD may be misinterpreted as shyness, disobedience, or even a lack of discipline. This often delays diagnosis and early intervention.

- **Increased Awareness**: In recent years, campaigns, improved diagnostic tools, and better-trained professionals have made it easier to identify autism. While this has led to more cases being reported, it doesn't necessarily mean autism is becoming more common—it's simply being recognized more often.

Message for Parents: Greater awareness benefits everyone. By advocating for understanding and access to resources, you're helping pave the way for earlier diagnoses and better outcomes in your community.

10. Prenatal Stress: The Quiet Contributor

Pregnancy is a time of immense physical and emotional change, but significant stress during this period can have subtle effects on a baby's development.

- **Emotional and Physical Stress**: High levels of maternal stress—caused by trauma, financial strain, or inadequate prenatal care—can influence the baby's developing brain, potentially increasing the risk of autism.

How to Reduce Stress:

- Practice mindfulness or prenatal yoga.

- Surround yourself with supportive friends and family.

- Seek medical guidance to address any concerns.

11. Nutritional Factors: The Role of Diet During Pregnancy

A healthy pregnancy diet isn't just about physical well-being—it's vital for brain development too.

- **Folate Deficiency**: Folate, found in leafy greens and prenatal vitamins, supports neural tube development. Low levels during pregnancy can impair fetal brain growth and increase the likelihood of developmental issues.

- **Vitamin D Deficiency**: Emerging research suggests that insufficient levels of vitamin D during pregnancy may contribute to autism risk. Sunlight and fortified foods are excellent sources.

Tips for Parents: Prenatal vitamins, a balanced diet, and regular checkups ensure you and your baby get the nutrients needed for optimal development.

12. 12. Screen Time and Environmental Stimulation: The Digital Dilemma

Modern parenting often involves navigating the role of technology, and while screens can be educational, they may pose risks when overused.

- **Early Exposure to Screens**: Excessive screen time in young children has been linked to delays in language and social development, which may mimic or exacerbate autism traits.

- **Lack of Interaction**: Babies learn best through human connection—eye contact, smiles, and play. Reduced opportunities for these interactions can hinder social and communication skills.

What Parents Can Do: Encourage hands-on play, outdoor activities, and face-to-face interaction. Reserve screen time for educational purposes and keep it minimal, especially during the first two years.

13. Birth Order: A Curious Connection

Some studies suggest a slight link between birth order and autism risk, though findings are inconsistent.

- **First-Born or Later-Born Children**: First-born children may face higher risks due to differences in parental age or prenatal care experience, while later-born children may encounter risks related to maternal health or shortened birth intervals.

What This Means: Birth order is just one small factor among many. Focus on your child's unique needs rather than statistical trends.

14. Associated Medical Conditions: Coexisting Challenges

Autism often overlaps with other medical conditions, which may shed light on its neurological underpinnings.

- **Seizure Disorders**: Epilepsy is more common in children with autism, suggesting shared pathways in brain development.

- **Gastrointestinal Issues**: Many children with autism experience digestive challenges, such as constipation or food sensitivities. While these issues don't cause autism, they can impact a child's overall well-being.

What Parents Can Do: Work with your child's healthcare provider to address co-occurring conditions, ensuring they have the best support for both their physical and developmental needs.

Reducing Risk and Early Diagnosis: What Parents Can Do

Understanding the factors that influence autism isn't about finding blame; it's about empowering parents to take proactive steps for their child's well-being. While many of these factors are beyond control, there are ways to create a supportive environment for your child's growth and development.

Prenatal Care: Building a Strong Foundation

A healthy pregnancy is the first step in supporting your child's development. Regular medical checkups allow healthcare providers to monitor your baby's growth and address any concerns early. Adding supplements like folic acid to your routine can promote healthy brain development, while prenatal vitamins ensure your baby gets all the nutrients they need.

Actionable Tip: Work closely with your doctor to create a prenatal care plan tailored to your needs.

Healthy Lifestyle Choices: What to Avoid

Simple lifestyle adjustments during pregnancy can make a big difference.

- **Avoid Smoking and Alcohol**: These substances can harm your baby's developing brain and increase the risk of complications.

- **Minimize Exposure to Harmful Chemicals**: Stay away from pesticides, heavy metals, and air pollutants. Opt for organic foods and safer cleaning products when possible.

Actionable Tip: Create a pregnancy-friendly environment by replacing harsh chemicals with natural alternatives and maintaining a balanced diet.

Final Thoughts for Parents and Caregivers

Risk factors for autism are not guarantees—they are pieces of a larger puzzle. Having one or more risk factors doesn't mean your child will develop autism, and many children with autism have no identifiable risk factors at all.

The most important thing is to focus on what you can control:

- Prioritize a healthy pregnancy through regular checkups and a balanced lifestyle.

- Monitor your child's developmental milestones and celebrate their progress.

- Take action early if concerns arise, as timely interventions can make a world of difference.

With the right support, children with autism can grow, learn, and thrive in ways that highlight their unique strengths. Every child is a world of potential waiting to unfold—and as a parent, you are their greatest advocate and guide. Together, you can navigate this journey with hope, confidence, and endless possibilities.

Chapter 4

Age-Wise Signs and Symptoms of Autism

A Story: Why Early Identification Matters

When Neha's son Aarush turned six months old, she noticed something different. Unlike other babies in her family who giggled at peek-a-boo or reached out eagerly for their favorite toys, Aarush seemed content staring at the ceiling fan. When Neha called his name, he didn't turn to her. "He's just an independent baby," well-meaning relatives assured her.

By the time Aarush was two years old, Neha's worries grew. He still wasn't saying "Mama" or pointing to objects like other toddlers. He spent hours spinning the wheels of his toy car but wouldn't join in when other kids played. A visit to a developmental pediatrician confirmed her suspicions—Aarush was diagnosed with Autism Spectrum Disorder (ASD).

Looking back, Neha wishes she'd known more about the early signs of autism. Acting sooner could have provided Aarush with earlier interventions and therapies to support his development. This story highlights why understanding the age-specific symptoms of autism is so crucial for parents. Early identification allows children to access resources that can transform their future.

Why Age-Specific Identification is Important

Autism presents differently at various stages of life. Recognizing these signs early equips parents to seek interventions tailored to their child's unique developmental needs. Let's explore the age-wise symptoms of autism and how they manifest across key developmental stages.

Age-Wise Signs and Symptoms of Autism

Understanding autism early is critical for timely intervention and support. Autism Spectrum Disorder (ASD) symptoms vary widely, but certain signs can be noticed as early as infancy and continue into later stages. These symptoms align with the DSM-5 criteria and focus on social communication, interaction, and restricted or repetitive behaviors.

Infants (0–12 Months): The Early Hints

Every parent eagerly watches for their baby's first smile, the way they light up when called by name, or the joy they express during playtime. For some babies with autism, these magical moments may appear delayed or absent, leaving parents puzzled or concerned.

- **Does not respond to their name**: By 6–9 months, most babies turn their heads eagerly when their name is called. A baby with autism might continue to focus on a toy or the ceiling fan, seemingly unaware.

- **Limited eye contact**: During feeding or cuddles, eye contact is a baby's way of bonding. Babies with autism might avoid looking into their caregiver's eyes, focusing on objects instead.

- **Lack of joyful expressions**: Smiling back at a smile is one of the earliest forms of connection. Babies with autism may not mirror this joy, leaving parents wondering why they don't react.

Behavioral Clues:

- **Quiet or overly passive**: While some babies cry frequently, others rarely seek attention or express their needs. This calm demeanor might seem like a blessing but it could be an early sign of autism.

Example: Aarav, as a baby, was unusually quiet. He didn't giggle at peek-a-boo or cry when hungry, preferring to stare at his mobile quietly for hours.

Toddlers (12–36 Months): Exploring the World, or Not?

As babies grow into toddlers, their world expands. They start pointing at airplanes, saying their first words, and exploring everything around them. For toddlers with autism, these developmental milestones might look a little different.

- **No meaningful words by 16 months**: While other toddlers chatter "Mama" or "Dada," a child with autism might use sounds instead of words or remain silent.

- **Does not point to show interest**: Most toddlers excitedly point to birds, airplanes, or toys to share their discoveries. Children with autism may skip this entirely, leaving parents puzzled by their lack of curiosity.

- **Avoids joint attention**: Toddlers usually love showing off their toys or sharing moments with their parents. For children with autism, this social connection might feel unnecessary.

- **Poor social engagement**: Simple gestures like waving goodbye or clapping might not come naturally, making them appear aloof or uninterested.

Behavioral Patterns:

- **Repetitive movements**: Hand flapping, toe walking, or spinning are common repetitive behaviors that may emerge in this stage.

- **Attachment to routines**: A change in the daily routine—like skipping a bath or eating at a different time—might cause distress.

- **Restricted play**: Instead of playing with a toy car by rolling it around, the child might obsess over spinning its wheels repeatedly.

Example: Aarush, at 18 months, would scream if his bedtime routine changed by even five minutes. While other toddlers enjoyed messy play, Aarush focused intensely on lining up toy blocks, never building anything with them.

Preschool Age (3–6 Years): When Differences Become Clearer

By preschool, children are learning to pretend, form friendships, and communicate their thoughts. For children with autism, these milestones can bring unique challenges that stand out more in group settings.

- **Does not engage in pretend play**: Pretending to cook in a toy kitchen or feeding a doll might not interest a child with autism. Instead, they may prefer repetitive actions, like stacking or sorting toys.

- **Speech delays or echolalia**: While some preschoolers may barely speak, others might echo words or phrases they've heard, such as lines from TV shows, without understanding their meaning.

- **Prefers to play alone**: Group play or peer interactions may hold little appeal. A child with autism might seem happier playing by themselves.

- **Lack of empathy or understanding**: Recognizing and responding to emotions, like comforting a crying friend, can be difficult for children with autism.

Behavioral Patterns:

- **Fascination with specific objects or topics**: Trains, numbers, dinosaurs, or even spinning fans might capture their attention for hours.

- **Sensory sensitivities**: Loud noises, bright lights, or certain textures can be overwhelming. For instance, they may refuse to wear scratchy clothes or eat crunchy foods.

- **Rigid routines**: Insisting on eating the same food every day or following a strict schedule is common and can lead to meltdowns if disrupted.

Example: Neha's daughter, Aanya, loved dinosaurs. She could name every type and their characteristics but refused to talk about anything else, even when friends tried to play house or draw with her.

School-Age Children (6–12 Years): Navigating Social and Academic Worlds

During the school years, children are expected to form friendships, follow routines, and engage in group activities. For children with autism, these expectations can bring unique challenges and strengths to light.

Social Communication and Interaction

- **Difficulty forming friendships**: While other children may bond over shared interests or games, a child with autism might prefer solitary activities like reading or collecting objects. They may struggle with initiating or maintaining friendships.

- **Literal understanding**: Subtle humor, sarcasm, or idioms might confuse them. For instance, a phrase like "break a leg" could lead to genuine concern.

- **Challenges in group settings**: Activities like group projects or playground games can be overwhelming, as they require turn-taking, sharing, and collaborative communication.

- **Monotone or robotic speech**: A child's speech may lack variation in tone or emotion, making it harder for peers to connect with them emotionally.

Behavioral Patterns

- **Obsessive interests**: A child might memorize every detail about dinosaurs or maps but show little interest in other subjects. These focused interests can be a source of pride and comfort.

- **Difficulty adapting to changes**: A substitute teacher, a schedule change, or even a new seating arrangement in class might trigger anxiety or resistance.

- **Motor mannerisms**: Behaviors like rocking, hand-flapping, or tapping may persist and act as self-soothing mechanisms.

Example: Rahul, a 10-year-old with autism, spent hours researching the weather in different countries. While his classmates played soccer, he preferred to share his findings with anyone willing to listen, often repeating the same facts enthusiastically.

Adolescents (13–18 Years): The Complexity of Teenage Years

The teenage years bring new social challenges and heightened expectations for independence. Adolescents with autism may find this transition particularly challenging, as they must navigate peer pressure, academic demands, and changes in their bodies and emotions.

Social Communication and Interaction

- **Struggles with social rules**: Understanding unspoken norms, like maintaining personal space or interpreting body language, can be difficult. For instance, they might stand too close during conversations or fail to recognize when someone is uncomfortable.

- **Challenges in building relationships**: Friendships may be limited or misunderstood. An adolescent might mistake a casual comment for deep interest or fail to notice when a peer is teasing.

- **Difficulty expressing emotions**: They may appear reserved or indifferent, even when feeling deeply about something. This can lead to misunderstandings with friends and family.

- **Struggles with sarcasm or abstract concepts**: Phrases like "it's raining cats and dogs" might be taken literally, leading to confusion.

Behavioral Patterns

- **Intense focus on specific hobbies or activities**: Whether it's collecting stamps, organizing trading cards, or researching a favorite historical event, these hobbies can become their primary focus.

- **Heightened anxiety**: Social anxiety, fear of new situations, or concerns about fitting in can become more pronounced.

- **Sensory sensitivities**: Preferences or aversions may persist, such as refusing certain clothing textures or avoiding noisy environments like crowded malls.

Example: Aanya, 15, loved astronomy and could name hundreds of constellations. While her classmates went to movies or parties, Aanya preferred spending her evenings with her telescope, avoiding loud or chaotic social settings.

Embracing Understanding and Taking Action

Recognizing the signs and symptoms of autism at different ages is not just about identifying challenges—it's about unlocking potential. Children and adolescents with autism experience the world differently, and these differences are what make them unique. Early identification allows parents to provide timely support, fostering their child's strengths while addressing areas of need.

As you reflect on the age-specific traits discussed in this chapter, remember that every child develops at their own pace. If you notice behaviors that stand out or delay milestones, trust your instincts and consult a professional. Autism is not a limitation but a spectrum of possibilities. By understanding and acting early, you can empower your child to navigate their world with confidence, curiosity, and joy. Embrace their individuality, celebrate their achievements, and be their unwavering advocate in this journey. The path may be different, but it is filled with extraordinary potential.

Chapter 5

A Detailed Understanding of Signs and Symptoms in Autism

A Mother's Search for Answers

When Ananya's three-year-old son, Ishaan, started showing unusual behaviors, she was determined to understand what was happening. Ishaan didn't point at airplanes in the sky like other children or bring her toys to share. He would spend hours spinning the wheels of his cars but avoided playing with his cousins.

Ananya sought answers online, reading every article she could find about autism. Some resources were too technical, filled with scientific jargon she couldn't decipher. Others were vague, offering little clarity about what to look for or how to help. Frustrated but determined, Ananya realized what she needed: clear, science-based information presented in a way she could understand and use.

This chapter is written for parents like Ananya. Using the widely recognized **DSM-5 criteria**, we'll explain autism's core characteristics—social communication challenges and restricted, repetitive behaviors—in simple terms with relatable examples. By the end, you'll have a detailed, practical understanding of what autism looks like and how to identify these traits in your child.

A. Understanding Social Communication Challenges in Autism

Imagine a world where sharing excitement or expressing emotions feels like solving a puzzle without a picture to guide you. For many children with Autism Spectrum Disorder (ASD), social communication can feel just like this—complex, overwhelming, and hard to navigate. Let's delve into what this looks like in real-life scenarios, so parents can better understand and support their children.

1. Social-Emotional Reciprocity: The Give-and-Take of Interaction

Social-emotional reciprocity is the natural back-and-forth in conversations and interactions that connects us to others. For children with autism, this flow may feel interrupted or one-sided.

Signs and Real-Life Examples:

- **Pointing to show interest**: Picture a family walk in the park. A typical child might excitedly point to a bird and say, "Look at the birdie!" to share their wonder. A child with autism, however, might watch silently, missing the opportunity to include others in their joy.

  What to Notice: Does your child point at objects to share their interest, like pointing to a plane in the sky or a flower in the garden?

- **Talking about likes or achievements**: Most children love to share their latest artwork or proudly show off a new skill. A child with autism might need prompting to share such moments, even if they are equally proud.

  What to Notice: Does your child talk about their interests or accomplishments without needing to be asked?

- **Preferring solitude over group play**: While many children delight in playing hide-and-seek or building sandcastles with friends, a child with autism may prefer lining up their toy cars or flipping through a picture book alone.

  What to Notice: Does your child avoid group activities or seem annoyed when others try to join their playtime?

2. Nonverbal Communication: The Unspoken Language

Nonverbal cues like eye contact, gestures, and facial expressions are critical for understanding and being understood. For children with autism, these nonverbal tools may not come naturally, making interactions feel disconnected.

Signs and Real-Life Examples:

- **Eye Contact**: Imagine asking your child, "Would you like some juice?" While most children look at your face to respond, a child with autism might stare at the juice box instead, making it harder to tell if they understood your question.

  What to Notice: Does your child make eye contact when asking for something, playing, or interacting with others?

- **Using gestures**: Waving goodbye, giving a high-five, or folding hands in a greeting like "namaste" are small but meaningful ways we connect. A child with autism may skip these gestures altogether, making their interactions seem less warm or responsive.

  What to Notice: Does your child naturally wave, clap, or use other gestures to communicate?

- **Facial expressions**: Imagine a child smiling brightly when they're upset or showing no reaction to a joke. This mismatch between emotions and expressions can confuse others, making social interactions challenging for a child with autism.

  What to Notice: Does your child's facial expressions match their emotions? For example, do they smile when they're happy or frown when they're upset?

3. Difficulty Developing and Maintaining Relationships

Friendships and social connections are essential for children, yet for those with autism, the process of forming and maintaining these bonds can be uniquely challenging.

Signs and Observations:

- **Enjoying the company of other children**:

Most children thrive on group play, sharing toys, or chatting with peers. A child with autism, however, might prefer solitary activities like lining up blocks or flipping through a picture book.

What to Observe: Does your child prefer playing alone even when others invite them to join? Do they move away when siblings or friends try to engage?

Example: Ayaan's classmates loved playing tag during recess, but he often stood at the edge of the playground, content to spin the wheels of his toy car instead.

- **Age-appropriate friendships**:

By age 4 or 5, most children form friendships with peers their own age. A child with autism might gravitate toward much younger or older children, or avoid forming bonds altogether.

What to Observe: Does your child connect with kids their age, or do they show more interest in significantly younger or older playmates?

Example: Meera, at age 6, loved spending time with her toddler cousin but found the games her classmates played overwhelming and confusing.

- **Understanding and following social rules**:

   Activities like board games or team sports require turn-taking, sharing, and following rules. Children with autism may find these expectations challenging, leading to frustration or withdrawal.

   What to Observe: Does your child understand the concept of taking turns in a game? Do they become upset when others don't follow the rules they've memorized?

   Example: While playing Ludo, Arjun insisted on everyone following the rules perfectly. If someone moved the wrong piece, he would get upset and leave the game.

B. Understanding Restricted and Repetitive Behaviors: A Window into Their World

For children with autism, repetitive actions and narrow interests are not just habits—they are coping mechanisms and sources of comfort. These behaviors provide structure and predictability in a world that often feels overwhelming.

1. Stereotyped or Repetitive Movements

Repetitive movements or speech patterns are common in autism, and they serve many purposes, from self-regulation to communication.

Examples:

- **Hand Flapping or Spinning**: A child might wave their hands when excited or spin in circles to express joy or relieve stress.

  Parent Observation: "When my daughter sees bubbles, she flaps her hands excitedly. It's her way of showing happiness."

- **Echolalia (Repeating Words)**: Instead of answering a question, a child may repeat the words or phrases they hear, like an echo.

  Parent Observation: "If I ask my son, 'Do you want milk?' he responds, 'Want milk? Want milk?' but doesn't answer yes or no."

  Example: Aarav loved a particular line from his favorite cartoon: "To infinity and beyond!" He repeated it frequently, especially when he was excited.

2. Insistence on Sameness: The Need for Predictability

For children with autism, routines and focused interests provide a sense of control and comfort in an otherwise unpredictable world. While these traits might seem puzzling or rigid to others, they are deeply meaningful and serve as anchors for stability and joy.

Imagine a world where every change feels like stepping onto shaky ground. For many children with autism, routines are not just preferences—they're essential for maintaining balance and security.

What This Looks Like:

- **Strict Routines**: A child with autism might insist on following the same sequence of events every day. Taking a different route to school, sitting at a new table for dinner, or even rearranging their toys can feel overwhelming and unsettling.

  Parent Observation: "If I drive a different way home, my child cries the entire ride and refuses to get out of the car once we arrive."

  Example: Aarush, a 5-year-old, insisted on eating his meals in the same order every day—rice first, then vegetables, and finally dessert. If the order was disrupted, he would refuse to eat altogether.

- **Distress Over Minor Changes**: Even seemingly small adjustments, like moving a favorite chair or using a different plate, can cause intense reactions.

  Example: Neha noticed her daughter, Aanya, would meltdown if her favorite green cup wasn't available for breakfast.

Why It Happens:

Routines offer predictability, helping children with autism feel safe in a world that might otherwise seem chaotic. Changes can trigger anxiety or frustration because they disrupt the sense of order these children rely on.

3. Highly Fixated Interests: A World of Fascination

Children with autism often develop intense interests in specific topics or objects. While these focused passions might seem unusual or excessive to others, they are a source of immense joy and knowledge for the child.

What This Looks Like:

- **Focused Interests**: A child may become deeply knowledgeable about a single topic, like dinosaurs, trains, or planets, and spend hours talking or thinking about it.

  Parent Observation: "My son knows every single dinosaur's name and can tell you where they lived and what they ate, but he struggles to talk about anything else."

  Example: Aryan, a 7-year-old, could recite entire train schedules and loved watching train videos online. He would enthusiastically share his knowledge, even when others didn't share the same level of interest.

- **Narrow Focus on Object Parts**: Instead of playing with toys as intended, children with autism might focus on specific features, like spinning wheels or shiny surfaces.

  Example: Kavya loved her toy cars but didn't "drive" them like her peers. Instead, she spent hours watching the wheels spin, captivated by the motion.

Why It Matters:

Focused interests can be a way for children to connect with the world, develop expertise, and find comfort in familiar topics. While these passions might seem narrow, they often reveal the child's unique strengths and potential.

4. The Sensory World of Autism

Imagine walking into a brightly lit supermarket where the fluorescent lights seem to buzz louder than conversations, the rough fabric of your sweater itches unbearably, and the strong smell of cleaning products feels suffocating. For a child with Autism Spectrum Disorder (ASD), these sensory experiences can be overwhelming, confusing, or even comforting, depending on how they perceive the world. Sensory sensitivities are a hallmark of autism and provide a glimpse into the unique ways children with ASD interact with their environment.

What Are Sensory Sensitivities?

Children with autism may experience sensory inputs—sound, touch, light, smell, taste, or temperature—differently from others. These sensitivities fall into two broad categories:

- **Over-Sensitivity (Hyper-Responsive)**: Where everyday stimuli feel intense and overwhelming.

- **Under-Sensitivity (Hypo-Responsive)**: Where a lack of reaction to stimuli can seem puzzling or concerning.

Understanding these responses is key to helping your child feel safe and comfortable in a sensory-rich world.

A. Over-Sensitivity (Hyper-Responsive)

For hyper-responsive children, sensory inputs can feel exaggerated, almost like turning up the volume or brightness to the highest setting.

Examples:

- **Sounds**: Loud or sudden noises, like a doorbell, vacuum cleaner, or fireworks, may feel unbearable.

  - *Parent Observation*: "Whenever I turn on the blender, my child covers their ears and runs out of the kitchen."

  - *Tip*: Use noise-canceling headphones to reduce sound intensity during activities like vacuuming.

- **Textures**: Certain fabrics or clothing tags can feel scratchy or irritating against their skin.

  - *Parent Observation*: "My daughter refuses to wear woolen sweaters and will only wear soft cotton clothes."

  - *Tip*: Choose seamless or tag-free clothing made from soft materials to keep your child comfortable.

- **Lights**: Bright or flickering lights, such as those in malls or supermarkets, can be distressing.

  - *Example*: "My child avoids brightly lit stores because the lights are too harsh."

  - *Tip*: Sunglasses or hats can help reduce discomfort in bright environments.

- **Touch**: Unexpected touches, like a pat on the back or a hug, may feel uncomfortable or even painful.

  - *Parent Observation*: "Whenever I hug my son, he stiffens up and pulls away."

  - *Tip*: Ask your child for permission before initiating physical contact and allow them to express their preferences.

B. Under-Sensitivity (Hypo-Responsive)

For hypo-responsive children, sensory inputs might seem muted, almost like turning the volume or brightness down too low.

Examples:

- **Sounds**: The child may not respond to their name being called or seem unaware of loud noises like a barking dog.

  - *Parent Observation*: "Even when the doorbell rings, my child doesn't react or look toward the door."

  - *Tip*: Use gentle physical cues, like a light touch on their arm, to capture their attention.

- **Pain or Temperature**: The child might not feel pain when injured or notice extreme temperatures.

  - *Example*: "My son fell off his bike, scraped his knee, and didn't cry or seem bothered."

  - *Tip*: Monitor for injuries or temperature-related issues, even if your child doesn't express discomfort.

- **Smell and Taste**: They may show a fascination with unusual smells or prefer strong, intense flavors.

  - *Parent Observation*: "My child smells her food before eating and loves extremely spicy or sour foods."

  - *Tip*: Embrace their sensory preferences while encouraging them to explore new tastes and smells gently.

- **Touch**: The child might seek out strong sensory input, like squeezing objects or pressing against walls.

  - *Example*: "My daughter loves squishing playdough and leans into firm hugs."

  - *Tip*: Provide sensory-friendly toys like stress balls or weighted blankets to meet their needs.

Understanding the Spectrum

It's important to remember that no two children with autism experience sensory sensitivities in the same way. One child might cover their ears at the sound of a vacuum, while another might not even react to a fire alarm. These variations are why autism is described as a "spectrum."

While sensory sensitivities may create challenges, they also highlight your child's unique way of perceiving the world. By observing and respecting these differences, you can create a supportive environment tailored to their needs.

The Power of Knowledge: How Understanding Autism Helps Parents Like Ananya

As Ananya closed the chapter, a wave of relief washed over her. The mystery of Ishaan's behaviors—his fascination with spinning wheels, his aversion to hugs, his need for routines—was no longer overwhelming or confusing. Now, she had clarity. Each of Ishaan's traits fit into a broader picture of Autism Spectrum Disorder (ASD), described in ways she could finally understand.

By recognizing the signs of autism early, Ananya realized she had taken the first and most important step in supporting Ishaan's growth. She learned how behaviors that once seemed puzzling were simply his unique way of navigating the world. Armed with accurate knowledge, Ananya felt empowered to seek interventions tailored to Ishaan's needs and strengths, steering clear of misinformation and myths.

For parents like Ananya, understanding autism is more than just gaining facts—it's about seeing their child's world with compassion and clarity. Early identification, as this chapter emphasized, is not just about diagnosis but about opening doors to possibilities, therapies, and support systems that can help every child thrive in their own extraordinary way.

Chapter 6

Co-Morbidities or Associations in Autism Spectrum Disorder (ASD): A Comprehensive Guide for Parents

A Parent's Journey: Recognizing the Bigger Picture

When Soniya's son Arjun was diagnosed with autism, she thought she had found the answers to his behaviors—his speech delays, repetitive movements, and preference for routine. But as time went on, Soniya noticed new challenges that weren't explained by autism alone. Arjun had trouble sleeping, would cry inconsolably after meals, and seemed anxious in new places. Desperate for clarity, Soniya asked, "Is this just autism, or is there more to it?"

Soniya's story is a familiar one for many parents. Autism Spectrum Disorder (ASD) often comes with additional medical, mental health, and developmental conditions, known as **co-morbidities**. These challenges can vary widely, but understanding them is key to addressing a child's holistic needs and improving their quality of life.

Medical Co-Morbidities in Autism: Stories for Parents

1.1 Epilepsy: The Silent Disruption

When four-year-old Aarav suddenly started zoning out during playtime, his mother, Meena, thought he was simply daydreaming. But then it happened during dinner—Aarav froze, staring blankly at his plate, unresponsive for what felt like an eternity. A few weeks later, Meena noticed a different episode: Aarav's arm jerked uncontrollably, and his body stiffened. Alarmed, she rushed him to a pediatrician, who diagnosed him with epilepsy.

Meena learned that epilepsy is common in children with autism and often begins in early childhood. With medication and regular check-ups, Aarav's seizures became manageable, allowing him to participate in therapy and enjoy his favorite activities.

Signs to Watch For:

- Staring spells or unresponsiveness.

- Jerking or stiffening movements.

- Loss of consciousness.

Parental Tip: If you notice these symptoms, consult a pediatrician. Early diagnosis and anti-epileptic drugs (AEDs) can make a significant difference.

1.2 Gastrointestinal (GI) Issues: The Hidden Pain

Six-year-old Anaya had always been a picky eater, but her mother, Shreya, began noticing unusual patterns. Anaya would cry uncontrollably after meals, clutching her stomach but unable to explain her pain. She often refused to eat, and her stools were either infrequent or unusually loose. Shreya initially thought it was just a phase, but the frequent meltdowns made her wonder if something deeper was wrong.

A visit to a pediatrician revealed that Anaya was suffering from gastrointestinal issues—a common challenge for children with autism. By addressing her dietary needs and introducing more fiber, along with eliminating certain food triggers, Anaya's discomfort lessened. Her mood improved, and she became more engaged in therapy.

Signs to Watch For:

- Constipation or diarrhea.

- Crying or withdrawal after meals.

- Unusual eating habits.

Parental Tip: Pay attention to your child's eating patterns and consult a pediatrician if problems persist. Dietary adjustments and medical support can significantly improve their comfort.

1.3 Sleep Disorders: Nights Without Rest

For Priya, bedtime was the hardest part of the day with her three-year-old son, Ishaan. While other children drifted off after a story, Ishaan would toss and turn for hours, often waking multiple times during the night. His restless sleep left him irritable and tired during the day, making therapy sessions and daily routines more challenging.

After consulting a pediatrician, Priya learned that sleep problems are common in children with autism. With a consistent bedtime routine—dim lights, calming activities, and no screens before bed—Ishaan's sleep began to improve. A low dose of melatonin, recommended by the doctor, also helped him settle more easily.

Signs to Watch For:

- Difficulty falling asleep or staying asleep.

- Frequent waking during the night.

- Daytime fatigue or irritability.

Parental Tip: Create a soothing bedtime routine and consult a sleep specialist if needed. Simple changes, like reducing sensory stimuli before bed, can make a world of difference.

2. Behavioral and Mental Health Co-Morbidities in Autism: Stories for Parents

2.1 Attention-Deficit/Hyperactivity Disorder (ADHD): The Constant Whirlwind

Meera was exhausted. Her seven-year-old son, Rohan, seemed like a whirlwind of energy that never stopped. He would jump from one activity to another, leaving a trail of chaos behind him. At school, his teacher often complained that Rohan struggled to stay in his seat, frequently interrupting the class with random outbursts. Even during therapy, Rohan's inability to focus made it hard for him to follow instructions.

When Meera shared her concerns with a developmental pediatrician, she learned that ADHD often co-occurs with autism. Understanding this, the family began behavioral therapy sessions to teach Rohan strategies for managing his impulses. With consistent reinforcement and, eventually, medication, Rohan started to focus better at school and home.

Signs to Watch For:

- Trouble finishing tasks or sitting still.

- Constant fidgeting or running around.

- Acting on impulses without thinking of the outcome.

Parental Tip: Behavioral therapy and structured routines can help children with ADHD. Medication may also provide additional support if recommended by a doctor.

2.2 Anxiety: The Fearful First Day

Nine-year-old Aarushi was anxious about her first day at a new school. While other children were excitedly choosing their backpacks, Aarushi spent hours pacing and asking repetitive questions: "Will the teacher be nice? Will they have lunch breaks? Will I get in trouble?" On the day itself, she refused to leave the house, complaining of a stomach ache and trembling.

Her mother, Priya, recognized this wasn't just ordinary nervousness but something deeper. After consulting a psychologist, Priya learned Aarushi's anxiety was linked to her autism, as children with ASD often struggle with change and uncertainty. Through Cognitive Behavioral Therapy (CBT) and gradual exposure to new situations, Aarushi slowly became more comfortable attending school.

Signs to Watch For:

- Avoiding unfamiliar situations or social settings.

- Repeatedly asking the same questions about fears.

- Physical symptoms like sweating, nausea, or trembling during stress.

Parental Tip: Teach relaxation techniques like deep breathing or using a weighted blanket. Occupational therapy can help address sensory triggers contributing to anxiety.

2.3 Depression: The Lost Spark

Thirteen-year-old Aditya used to love drawing. He would spend hours sketching animals and creating imaginary worlds. But over the past few months, he had stopped picking up his pencils. He spent most of his time alone in his room, refusing to eat dinner with the family or talk to his friends. When his mother, Sunita, asked if anything was wrong, Aditya shrugged and said, "I don't know."

Concerned, Sunita took him to a psychologist, who diagnosed Aditya with depression—a condition more common in older children and teens with autism. With therapy and support from his family, Aditya began expressing his feelings and gradually rediscovered his love for art.

Signs to Watch For:

- Withdrawal from favorite activities or people.

- Persistent sadness or irritability.

- Changes in sleep or appetite patterns.

Parental Tip: Recognize the signs early and consult a psychologist or psychiatrist. Therapy, and if needed, medication, can help your child regain their emotional balance.

3. Developmental Issues commonly associated with Autism: Stories for Parents

3.1 Intellectual Disabilities: A Journey of Small Victories

Amit was worried about his five-year-old daughter, Maya. While her cousins of the same age could recite nursery rhymes and count to 10, Maya struggled to name colors or remember the sequence of days in a week. She often needed help with simple self-care tasks, like dressing or eating with a spoon.

When Maya's preschool teacher mentioned her struggles in class, Amit sought help from a developmental pediatrician. After assessments, Maya was found to have an intellectual disability along with autism. The doctor explained that while Maya's learning might take longer, early intervention and an Individualized Education Plan (IEP) could help her progress.

With the support of special educators and tailored learning strategies, Maya began to show improvements. While she learned at her own pace, every small milestone—naming her favorite colors or putting on her shoes—was a cause for celebration.

Signs to Watch For:

- Significant delays in developmental milestones like problem-solving or speaking.

- Difficulty with academic concepts like reading or math.

- Trouble performing age-appropriate tasks like getting dressed or using utensils.

Parental Tip: Work closely with schools to create IEPs and celebrate small victories. Early intervention programs can make a significant difference.

3.2 Speech and Language Delays: The First Words

Rhea was overjoyed when her son, Aarav, said his first word, "Mama," at nine months old. But by the time he turned two, Aarav wasn't using other words or forming sentences. Instead, he repeated lines from his favorite cartoon shows, like, "To infinity and beyond!" without context. At playdates, other toddlers chatted away while Aarav remained silent, leaving Rhea feeling isolated and concerned.

A speech-language pathologist assessed Aarav and identified both autism and speech delays. They began regular speech therapy, using visual aids like picture cards to encourage communication. Slowly but steadily, Aarav learned to express his needs, starting with pointing at pictures and eventually stringing words together.

Signs to Watch For:

- No words by 18 months or very limited vocabulary by age 2.

- Difficulty forming meaningful sentences or answering questions.

- Repeating phrases (echolalia) instead of using language for communication.

Parental Tip: Speech therapy can unlock your child's ability to communicate. Consider using tools like picture exchange systems or apps to bridge the gap.

3.3 Motor Challenges: Small Steps to Big Achievements

At age six, Arjun loved playing with his toy cars but avoided climbing on playground structures or riding a bike with his friends. His parents noticed that even holding a crayon or using scissors was hard for him, and his handwriting was nearly illegible. Arjun seemed frustrated when he couldn't keep up with his peers.

A therapist explained that Arjun's autism included motor challenges that affected both fine and gross motor skills. With the help of occupational and physical therapy, Arjun began to build strength and coordination. Over time, he learned to zip up his jacket, hold a pencil properly, and even ride a tricycle—a moment that brought tears of joy to his parents' eyes.

Signs to Watch For:

- Struggles with physical coordination, such as climbing, running, or jumping.

- Difficulty with fine motor tasks like handwriting or using scissors.

- Frustration with activities requiring both focus and dexterity.

Parental Tip: Therapies focused on motor skills can improve coordination and build confidence. Celebrate every milestone, no matter how small.

4. Feeding and Eating Disorders: Beyond the Plate

Meera's mornings were a battle. Her four-year-old son, Kabir, insisted on eating only plain rice for breakfast. Any attempt to offer something different—fruit, bread, or eggs—was met with tears and tantrums. Kabir's food preferences extended to lunch and dinner, where he refused to eat anything but white-colored foods like pasta without sauce or boiled potatoes.

Meera was worried about his nutrition but didn't know where to start. After consulting a dietitian, she learned that Kabir's autism affected his sensory processing, making certain textures and tastes overwhelming for him. Together, they worked on gradually introducing new foods through playful activities like food art and allowing Kabir to explore different textures without pressure to eat them immediately. Slowly, Kabir began to accept new foods, starting with colorful fruits like bananas and oranges.

Signs to Watch For:

- Eating only specific foods, often limited by color, texture, or taste.

- Strong aversions to trying new foods or refusal to eat certain textures.

Parental Tip: Consult a dietitian who specializes in pediatric feeding challenges. Start with small steps, like introducing similar textures or mixing new foods with familiar ones.

5. Immune and Autoimmune Conditions: The Hidden Layer

Aditi was no stranger to sleepless nights. Her seven-year-old daughter, Rhea, was frequently unwell with colds, skin rashes, or stomach upsets. Aditi noticed that Rhea's eczema flared up during stressful periods, and she often seemed fatigued, even after a full night's sleep.

After speaking with a pediatrician, Aditi learned that children with autism sometimes have immune system irregularities, which can lead to frequent infections or conditions like asthma and eczema. With a tailored plan, including allergy tests, a balanced diet, and prescribed medications, Aditi was able to manage Rhea's symptoms effectively. She also incorporated gentle mindfulness practices to help Rhea handle stress, reducing flare-ups.

Signs to Watch For:

- Chronic issues like frequent colds, rashes, or allergies.

- Symptoms of autoimmune conditions, such as asthma or persistent inflammation.

Parental Tip: Work closely with a pediatrician to identify triggers and manage symptoms. Keeping a health diary can help track patterns and potential irritants.

Challenges in Identifying Co-Morbidities: Listening Beyond Words

Eight-year-old Aarush's teacher noticed he was increasingly irritable during class and often put his head on the desk. At home, Aarush began having more meltdowns, but he couldn't articulate what was wrong. His parents initially thought it was anxiety from a recent change in his school schedule. However, a visit to a pediatrician revealed that Aarush had chronic gastrointestinal discomfort, likely causing his mood swings and fatigue.

This situation taught Aarush's parents that children with autism may express discomfort through behaviors rather than words. They learned to watch for subtle cues, like changes in sleep patterns or increased irritability, as signs that something might be wrong.

Challenges to Recognize:

- Difficulty verbalizing physical or emotional discomfort.

- Behaviors like meltdowns, withdrawal, or sleep disturbances as signs of underlying conditions.

Parental Tip: Trust your instincts and observe behavioral changes closely. Seek medical advice when something feels off, even if your child cannot explain their discomfort.

A Journey Toward Understanding Co-Morbidities

When Soniya began to recognize the connections between Arjun's frequent tantrums, his sleepless nights, and his refusal to eat certain foods, a lightbulb moment occurred. She realized that his struggles weren't just a part of his autism but pointed to co-morbidities needing attention. Armed with the knowledge from her pediatrician and resources like this chapter, she no longer felt helpless. Instead, she felt empowered.

By understanding co-morbidities and associations, parents like Soniya can become more attuned to their children's needs, bridging gaps that might have been overlooked. Every challenge—whether a GI issue, anxiety, or feeding aversion—holds an answer when addressed thoughtfully.

This journey of awareness doesn't just improve the child's quality of life but also strengthens the bond between parent and child. When parents listen beyond words, observe behaviors closely, and act with compassion, they pave the way for a brighter, healthier future for their children.

Chapter 7

The First Steps: What to Do When Autism Becomes a Question

A Story of Uncertainty and Determination

Meera sat at the park, watching other toddlers chatter, laugh, and chase after butterflies. Her son, Aarav, sat nearby, completely absorbed in spinning the wheels of his toy car. He didn't respond when she called his name. "Maybe he's just shy," she told herself, echoing the reassurances from friends and family. But deep down, Meera felt something was different. Aarav rarely looked her in the eye or pointed to things he wanted. He didn't babble like other kids his age. Was this just a phase? Or was it something more?

Overwhelmed by worry, Meera began searching for answers. Her internet search brought her a flood of information—some helpful, some conflicting, and some that only added to her confusion. She asked herself, "Who do I approach? How do I explain my concerns? Will anyone take me seriously?"

This chapter is for parents like Meera, who sense that something is different about their child but aren't sure how to navigate the journey. It's about breaking down the steps to understanding autism, seeking the right help, and finding answers based on evidence, not myths. Let's explore how early action and professional guidance can make all the difference for your child's future.

Why Early Action Matters

Taking the first steps when you notice signs of Autism Spectrum Disorder (ASD) can feel daunting. But acting early can unlock opportunities for your child to thrive and ensure they receive the support they need.

Benefits of Early Diagnosis:

- Early interventions, such as speech or occupational therapy, can significantly improve skills like communication and social interaction.

- Understanding your child's unique needs helps you provide better support, reducing frustration for both you and your child.

- Addressing developmental delays early can lead to better long-term outcomes, from learning abilities to emotional well-being.

Addressing Parental Concerns: It's normal to feel uncertain or even deny the possibility of autism at first. Seeking professional advice helps clarify whether your child is experiencing typical development or needs additional support. Remember, early action is about empowering your child, no matter the diagnosis.

What to Expect During the Visit: A Journey to Clarity

Walking into the pediatrician's office, many parents feel a mix of hope and apprehension. You've noticed behaviors that feel different, and now you're taking a brave first step to seek clarity. What happens next can provide valuable insights into your child's development.

During the visit, your pediatrician will not only listen to your concerns but also observe how your child interacts with you and the environment. This isn't just about quick observations—it's about piecing together a puzzle:

- **Watching Interactions**: Does your child respond when their name is called? Do they engage with toys or objects?

- **Asking Questions**: Your pediatrician will inquire about speech development, social behaviors, and responses to sensory inputs like loud noises or touch.

- **Referrals if Needed**: Based on these observations, your pediatrician might suggest seeing a specialist, such as a developmental pediatrician, psychologist, or neurologist, for a deeper assessment.

Example: A pediatrician may notice that your child avoids eye contact or prefers playing alone. These subtle cues could prompt a referral for further evaluation, opening the door to understanding your child better.

Screening Tests for Autism: Shining a Light on Developmental Differences

Screening tests are like the first gentle taps on a door that might lead to a larger conversation about your child's development. They're not meant to diagnose autism but rather to identify children who might need a closer look.

Purpose of Screening

Screening helps distinguish between typical developmental differences and potential delays. Even if a child doesn't show obvious signs, screening ensures that no concerns go unnoticed.

Available Screening Tools

Here are two tools commonly used by professionals to screen for autism:

1. **M-CHAT-R/F (Modified Checklist for Autism in Toddlers, Revised with Follow-Up)**

   - **Age Range**: Ideal for children aged 16 to 30 months.

   - **Purpose**: Detects early signs of autism through a simple parent-completed questionnaire.

   - **How It Works**:

     - Parents answer questions about their child's behavior. For example, does your child respond to their name or point to show you something interesting?

     - A follow-up discussion with your pediatrician may clarify responses if concerns arise.

Example Question: "Does your child use their finger to point at objects to share interest, like pointing at an airplane in the sky?"

2. **Trivandrum Autism Behaviour Checklist (TABC)**

- **Age Range**: Designed for children aged 2 to 6 years, focusing on the crucial early childhood development stages.

- **Purpose**: Screens for behavioral markers associated with Autism Spectrum Disorder (ASD).

- **How It Works**:

   - The checklist evaluates behaviors across areas like social interaction, communication, sensory responses, and repetitive movements.

   - Caregivers answer questions about the frequency of specific behaviors, such as "Does your child resist changes in routine?"

   - The results guide referrals for detailed diagnostic assessments and interventions.

Example Behaviors: A child who avoids eye contact or engages in repetitive hand movements like flapping could show signs that warrant further evaluation.

What Happens After Screening? The Next Steps in Understanding

Whether the screening results are positive or negative, they serve as a compass guiding you forward:

1. **Positive Results**:

   - If the screening suggests signs of autism, your pediatrician will recommend further evaluations with specialists.

   - Specialists may use detailed diagnostic tools to confirm autism and assess its severity.

2. **Negative Results**:

   - Even if the screening doesn't indicate autism, don't hesitate to voice lingering concerns. Not all developmental delays fall under autism but may still require support and interventions.

Reassurance for Parents: A positive screening result doesn't confirm autism, and a negative result doesn't dismiss your concerns. Trust your instincts as a parent—this is only the first step in understanding and supporting your child. Screening is a tool, not the final answer.

The Process of Definitive Diagnosis: Turning Uncertainty into Clarity

Imagine being in a room full of puzzle pieces, trying to fit them together without knowing the final picture. This is how many parents feel when they first notice signs of Autism Spectrum Disorder (ASD) in their child. Seeking a definitive diagnosis is like finding the missing corner pieces—it brings clarity, direction, and the foundation to understand your child's unique needs.

Why Diagnosis is the Key

A definitive diagnosis doesn't just confirm whether a child has autism; it acts as a blueprint for understanding their challenges and strengths. It helps parents plan appropriate interventions and access the right support systems to improve their child's quality of life.

Diagnostic Criteria: The Role of DSM-5

What is DSM-5?

The **Diagnostic and Statistical Manual of Mental Disorders, 5th Edition (DSM-5)** is the gold standard generally used by healthcare professionals worldwide to diagnose autism. It ensures consistency in evaluation and offers clear criteria for identifying autism traits.

Key Areas Assessed

1. **Deficits in Social Communication and Interaction**

   - **Example**: Your child might struggle to understand nonverbal cues, such as a friend crossing their arms to signal discomfort, or have difficulty making friends.

   - **What to Watch For**: Limited back-and-forth conversations, challenges in sharing emotions, and difficulty understanding social norms.

2. **Restricted and Repetitive Behaviors, Interests, or Activities**

   - **Example**: Repetitive hand-flapping when excited or distress over changes in routine, such as moving dinner from the kitchen to the dining room.

   - **What to Watch For**: Intense focus on specific interests (e.g., trains, numbers), resistance to changes, and unusual sensory responses (e.g., covering ears at the sound of a blender).

These criteria help professionals identify whether a child's behavior fits the autism spectrum or points to other conditions requiring different support.

Who Makes the Diagnosis? The Role of Specialists

Diagnosing autism requires a team effort, with experts who understand the nuances of child development:

- **Developmental Pediatricians**: Specialists in identifying developmental delays and tracking progress.

- **Child Psychologists and Psychiatrists**: Experts in evaluating behavioral and mental health concerns.

- **Pediatric Neurologists**: Ensure that conditions like epilepsy or other neurological disorders aren't causing similar symptoms.

How They Diagnose

Through detailed observations, interviews with parents, and screening tools, these professionals piece together the child's developmental profile. Your insights as a parent—how your child interacts at home, reacts to changes, and communicates—play a vital role in this process.

A Diagnostic Tool with an Indian Lens: AIIMS Modified INDT-ASD

Why It's Unique

Imagine a tool designed not just to diagnose autism but to do so while embracing the unique cultural fabric of India. The **AIIMS Modified Indian Scale for Assessment of Autism (INDT-ASD)** achieves exactly that. While the globally recognized **DSM-5** framework provides a robust baseline, this Indian-specific tool ensures that behaviors and traits influenced by cultural and societal norms are carefully considered. It's like having a tailor-made lens that sees the child within their environment.

Key Features of the AIIMS Modified IN-DT-ASD

1. **Behavior-Specific Focus:**

   - It examines core autism traits like communication challenges, social reciprocity, repetitive behaviors, and sensory sensitivities.

   - Examples include whether a child points to objects to draw attention or how they respond to daily routines.

2. **Cultural Sensitivity:**

   - Unique family traditions and societal norms, such as greeting with a "Namaste" are incorporated into the tool to ensure behaviors are interpreted correctly.

3. **Tailored Observations**:

   - The tool leverages both parental input and professional observation, ensuring that discrepancies between the two are resolved through detailed follow-ups.

Understanding Severity: Scoring with ISAA and CARS

Once autism is identified, the next crucial step is understanding its severity. This is not just a technical exercise—it's the foundation for creating tailored interventions that match the child's unique needs. Tools like the **Indian Scale for Assessment of Autism (ISAA)** and the **Childhood Autism Rating Scale (CARS)** play a vital role in this process.

ISAA: An Indian Perspective on Autism Severity

ISAA is uniquely designed for the Indian context. It evaluates the child's behaviors through **40 items**, divided across six domains: **social relationships, emotional responsiveness, communication, behavior patterns, sensory aspects, and cognitive components**.

- **How It Works**: ISAA relies on detailed observations by trained professionals, complemented by input from caregivers. For example, they might assess how the child responds to social cues or their ability to communicate through gestures. Each behavior is rated on a 5-point scale, from "rarely" to "always," translating into a quantitative score.

- **Why It Matters**: ISAA not only measures severity but also determines eligibility for disability benefits in India. The scoring is categorized into **mild (70–106)**, **moderate (107–153)**, and **severe autism (154 and above)**.

CARS: A Global Measure of Autism

The **Childhood Autism Rating Scale (CARS)** is a widely recognized tool that evaluates **15 areas** of behavior, including social responses, communication, and sensory reactions.

- **How It Works**: Professionals score each domain on a scale from 1 to 4, observing how the child interacts with people, objects, and the environment. For instance, CARS assesses verbal and nonverbal communication by analyzing the child's use of speech and gestures.

- **Why It's Helpful**: CARS provides a clear interpretation of severity, with scores categorized as **mild to moderate (30–36)** and **severe (37+)** autism. It's a universal tool, ideal for planning globally standardized interventions.

A Mother's Clarity

Sitting in the waiting room of the developmental pediatrician, Meera clutched her notebook, filled with observations of Aarav's unique behaviors. The journey from doubt to action hadn't been easy. She remembered the days of sitting in the park, watching other toddlers giggle and play, and feeling the weight of uncertainty. But today, Meera felt different—empowered, informed, and ready to understand her son's world.

When the specialists completed Aarav's assessments using tools like the **AIIMS Modified INDT-ASD, ISAA,** and **CARS,** Meera was relieved to finally have clarity. The evaluations not only confirmed Aarav's autism but also provided insights into his strengths and challenges. She learned that while he needed support for his communication and social interactions, his intense focus on patterns and love for numbers could be nurtured into strengths.

The diagnosis wasn't an end—it was the beginning of a tailored plan to help Aarav thrive. With early interventions and resources, Meera felt confident about the path ahead. She realized that taking those first steps—listening to her instincts and seeking professional guidance—was the best decision for her son's future.

For parents like Meera, understanding autism is more than labels or charts. It's about embracing your child's uniqueness and unlocking their potential with the right tools and support. The journey may be challenging, but every step brings you closer to helping your child shine.

Chapter 8

Parenting in Autism: A Journey of Love and Resilience

A Story of Maya and Rohit: Navigating Uncertainty

Maya's mornings were a whirlwind of emotions. Her three-year-old son, Rohit, wasn't like other children his age. He preferred lining up his toy cars in perfect rows over playing with his cousins. He didn't wave goodbye to his grandparents or respond to his name when called. Maya often found herself wondering, "Is it just his personality, or is there something more?"

Friends offered well-meaning reassurances, saying he was just "quiet" or "independent." But Maya couldn't shake the feeling that something was different. Every tantrum in public or Rohit's meltdown over small changes in his routine left her feeling overwhelmed and isolated. Desperate for answers, Maya embarked on a journey of research, consultations, and learning to understand her son's unique world.

This chapter is for parents like Maya, navigating the unknown while wanting the best for their child. Parenting a child with Autism Spectrum Disorder (ASD) can feel like stepping into uncharted territory, but with the right tools, support, and mindset, it can also be a deeply fulfilling journey. Let's explore the joys, challenges, and strategies that can guide you along the way.

The Early Stages: Recognizing and Coping with Diagnosis

Early Concerns: Listening to the Whisper of Intuition

For many parents, the early signs of autism can feel like pieces of a puzzle that don't quite fit. A mother might notice her six-month-old not responding to their name, or a father might feel puzzled when his baby avoids making eye contact during playtime. These differences, subtle at first, often leave parents second-guessing their instincts.

Take Rhea, for instance. At nine months, her son Kabir wasn't babbling or pointing like other babies in their playgroup. Family members reassured her, saying, "He'll catch up," but deep down, Rhea felt something was different. It wasn't until Kabir turned three that a pediatrician confirmed her concerns—it was autism.

Parental Tip: Trust your instincts. You know your child best. If something feels off, consult a pediatrician or developmental specialist promptly. Early intervention can work wonders.

Relief and Challenges Post-Diagnosis: A Double-Edged Sword

The moment you receive an autism diagnosis, clarity and uncertainty arrive hand in hand. On one side, there's relief in understanding why your child behaves a certain way. On the other, the weight of the unknown future looms large.

For Rhea, the diagnosis brought mixed emotions. "Finally, I had a name for what we were facing," she said. "But what now? How do I help my son?" The journey from diagnosis to action can feel daunting, but it is also empowering.

Parental Tip: Focus on understanding your child's unique strengths and challenges. Education is your greatest ally—learn about autism and the resources available to help your child thrive.

Daily Life with Autism: Finding Balance in the Chaos

Parenting Stress: The Unseen Weight

Parenting a child with autism often means navigating uncharted waters. Everyday routines can feel like Herculean tasks, with meltdowns, communication barriers, and constant vigilance becoming part of the norm.

Imagine Neha's daily life with her daughter, Aanya. Simple outings to the park could turn into overwhelming experiences, as Aanya would freeze at the sound of barking dogs or melt down when another child touched her toy. Neha's exhaustion wasn't just physical—it was emotional too.

Practical Tips:

1. **Create a Routine:** A predictable schedule gives children with autism a sense of security and helps prevent meltdowns.

2. **Seek Support:** Connect with local or online support groups where parents share advice and encouragement.

3. **Celebrate Small Wins:** Every milestone, no matter how small, deserves to be celebrated. These moments are reminders of your child's progress.

Building Parent-Child Relationships: The Language of Love

Even without words, the bond between a parent and child can be profound. Children with autism may not always express affection in conventional ways, but their love often shines through in unique and beautiful moments.

A mother once shared, "My son doesn't say 'I love you,' but his big grin when he hears my voice is enough to melt my heart." For parents, these fleeting moments of connection become their most cherished memories.

Parental Tip: Look for your child's unique ways of showing love—a hug, a glance, or even a shared laugh—and respond with patience and understanding. These bonds will become your anchor through the challenges.

The Ripple Effect: Autism's Impact on Families

Siblings: Balancing Love and Challenges

For siblings of children with autism, the journey can be bittersweet. On one hand, they develop empathy and patience beyond their years. On the other, they may feel overlooked as their parents devote extra time and energy to their sibling's needs. Imagine Riya, a 10-year-old whose younger brother, Aarush, struggles with meltdowns in public. At times, Riya feels embarrassed, wishing her family could have a "normal" outing. Yet, she's fiercely protective of him when anyone else questions his behavior.

Parental Tip: Include siblings in conversations about autism. Explain why their sibling may act differently, and validate their feelings—both positive and negative. Engage them in activities where they can bond with their sibling, fostering understanding and love.

Marriages Under Pressure: The Silent Strain

The demands of parenting a child with autism can take a toll on marital relationships. Late nights navigating meltdowns, financial stress, and limited time for each other can increase tensions. For Ankit and Priya, raising their son with autism meant fewer date nights and more late-night discussions about therapies and routines. While they sometimes felt like partners in a business rather than a marriage, open communication helped them stay connected.

Parental Tip: Carve out time for your relationship, even if it's just a quiet cup of tea together after bedtime. Seeking counseling or therapy can also provide tools to navigate shared challenges and strengthen your bond.

Looking Ahead: Long-Term Concerns

The Lifelong Parenting Role

For many parents, autism doesn't just shape childhood—it redefines the future. Anil, father to 16-year-old Raj, spends sleepless nights worrying about what will happen after he's gone. "Who will ensure he's cared for? Will he have friends, a job, or a safe place to live?" These concerns weigh heavily on many parents as they navigate adulthood alongside their child.

Parental Tip: Begin planning early. Explore long-term care options, such as special needs trusts, legal guardianship, or assisted living communities. Planning today ensures peace of mind for tomorrow.

Caregiver Burnout: The Hidden Toll

The constant demands of caregiving can leave parents feeling physically and emotionally drained. For Meera, whose days revolved around her son's therapy sessions and meltdowns, exhaustion became her constant companion. She realized she needed to care for herself, too, to be the best parent she could be.

Parental Tip: Self-care isn't selfish—it's essential. Even a 15-minute walk or a quiet moment with a book can recharge your batteries. Don't hesitate to ask for help from family, friends, or respite care services.

Navigating Financial and Social Hurdles

Financial Strain

Therapy sessions, specialized education, and medical bills can pile up quickly, creating financial stress. Ankur and Kavya, parents of a child with autism, found themselves juggling expenses and searching for affordable support options.

Parental Tip: Research government programs, grants, or scholarships for children with special needs. Local autism organizations often have resources to help families manage costs effectively.

Breaking Social Isolation

Many parents feel cut off from their social circles due to their child's unique needs. Public outings can feel daunting, and friendships sometimes fade as priorities shift. Yet, connections are vital for emotional health.

Parental Tip: Seek out a support network of understanding friends, family, and professionals. Join local or online autism communities where you can share experiences and find companionship with others who truly understand the journey.

Finding Strength and Joy: Mental Health and Support in the Autism Journey

Mental Health: Navigating the Emotional Terrain

Parenting a child with autism is both a labor of love and a test of resilience. The emotional demands can feel overwhelming at times, especially for mothers, who often report bearing the brunt of caregiving stress. Yet, amidst the exhaustion and worry, there is a path toward balance and emotional well-being.

Impact on Mental Health

Imagine juggling therapy appointments, meltdowns, and sleepless nights, all while striving to maintain normalcy for the rest of the family. It's no wonder that anxiety and depression are common among parents of children with autism. But every challenge is an opportunity for growth.

Coping Tips:

- **Focus on Positives:** Celebrate the moments when your child learns something new or expresses love in their unique way. Their small victories are monumental.

- **Seek Therapy:** A counselor can provide tools to navigate emotional challenges and offer a safe space to share your struggles.

- **Practice Self-Care:** Whether it's a morning walk, yoga, or even five minutes of deep breathing, self-care isn't optional— it's necessary.

Resources and Support: Your Lifeline

No one should walk this path alone. A wealth of resources and support networks are available to help lighten the load and offer guidance.

Professional Guidance:

Therapists and specialists are like navigators in your journey. Speech therapists can unlock your child's communication, occupational therapists can help with sensory challenges, and behavioral specialists can address social and emotional growth.

Parental Tip: Stay proactive by regularly consulting these professionals to fine-tune your child's care plan.

Community Connections:

In the isolating moments, connecting with others who understand can be life-changing. Join local or online autism support groups to share experiences, advice, and even laughter. Attend workshops to learn strategies that empower you as an advocate for your child.

Example: One parent shared, "Hearing another mom talk about her son's progress gave me the hope I desperately needed on a tough day."

Discovering the Joys: Seeing the World Through a Different Lens

Amidst the challenges, there's unparalleled joy in parenting a child with autism. Their unique perspective on the world often brings surprising beauty and creativity to everyday life.

A Mother's Story:

"My daughter has a way of seeing patterns in nature that I would have never noticed. Her passion for drawing butterflies has brought us closer and filled our home with art and color."

Parental Tip: Celebrate your child's individuality. Their strengths—whether it's an artistic eye, an encyclopedic knowledge of dinosaurs, or a kind heart—are gifts that enrich your family's life.

Closing Thoughts: Love, Resilience, and Growth

Parenting a child with autism is not a journey you take alone. It's a shared path where every challenge is matched with support, and every step forward is celebrated. By nurturing your own mental health, tapping into available resources, and embracing the unique joys your child brings, you create an environment where both you and your child can thrive. Remember, help is always within reach—whether it's from a professional, a community, or even a kindred spirit sharing a similar story.

Chapter 9

Nurturing Growth: A Guide to Developmental Therapy in Autism

Finding Hope in Confusion: A Story

Priya and Raj had always been hands-on parents, but raising their three-year-old son, Aarav, felt different. Aarav didn't seem interested in playing with other children at the park. He rarely made eye contact and preferred lining up his toys to engaging in imaginative play. Priya and Raj found themselves in a whirlwind of questions:

"How can we help Aarav connect with us better?"

"What activities will support his learning at home?"

"Are we doing enough?"

Despite their love for their child, Priya and Raj felt unsure of how to support Aarav's development. Like many parents of children with autism, they sought guidance to make sense of his unique behaviors and unlock his potential.

Introduction to Developmental Therapy

What is Developmental Therapy?

Developmental therapy is a structured, child-centered approach that helps children with Autism Spectrum Disorder (ASD) build skills in communication, social interaction, motor development, and self-regulation. Instead of focusing solely on deficits, this approach emphasizes meeting children where they are developmentally and fostering their individual strengths.

Goals of Developmental Therapy

1. **Enhancing Communication:**

   Helping children express their needs and feelings through verbal or non-verbal means.

   - *Example:* Teaching a child to use pictures to request water when they cannot yet say the word.

2. **Building Social Interaction Skills:**

Encouraging meaningful connections with family, peers, and caregivers.

- *Example:* Practicing turn-taking during simple games like rolling a ball back and forth.

3. **Supporting Emotional Regulation:**

Teaching children to manage frustration, sensory overload, or anxiety.

- *Example:* Guiding a child to use deep breathing techniques during meltdowns.

4. **Fostering Independence:**

Developing life skills for daily activities such as dressing, eating, and cleaning up.

- *Example:* Encouraging a child to zip their jacket while providing support when needed.

The Heart of Home-Based Interventions: Why They Matter

Imagine your child learning in the place where they feel most comfortable—your home. For children with autism, home isn't just where they sleep and eat; it's their safe haven. Turning this familiar environment into a nurturing space for developmental therapy can make all the difference.

The Power of Parents: Everyday Heroes in Therapy

Parents are a child's first and most consistent teachers. With developmental therapy, they can transform everyday moments into valuable learning opportunities. Whether it's during mealtime, playtime, or even bedtime routines, these moments become building blocks for essential skills.

Key Benefits of Home-Based Therapy

1. A Familiar Environment

Children with autism often find new settings overwhelming. The bright lights of a therapy center, unfamiliar sounds, or new people can create unnecessary stress. Home-based therapy leverages the comfort of their safe space, allowing children to focus on learning without added anxiety.

Example: Practicing verbal requests at the dining table feels less intimidating than doing so in a clinical environment.

2. Consistency Brings Results

Learning is all about repetition, and what better place to reinforce skills daily than at home? When therapeutic strategies are practiced consistently, children are more likely to retain and apply what they learn.

Example: If a child is learning to take turns during play, parents can reinforce this skill every day, turning games into a consistent learning opportunity.

3. Flexibility That Fits Your Family

Home-based therapy can be customized to fit both the family's schedule and the child's unique needs. Parents can focus on the areas that matter most while weaving therapy seamlessly into daily routines.

Example: A child struggling with transitions can practice cleaning up toys after playtime, preparing them for smoother bedtime or school transitions.

A Journey of Growth for the Entire Family

Home-based therapy does more than help children thrive—it transforms families. By actively participating in therapy, parents gain a deeper understanding of their child's world, creating a stronger bond through shared victories.

Each small step, whether it's a newly learned word or a shared smile, becomes a milestone worth celebrating. Through this approach, parents evolve from caregivers to active partners in their child's developmental journey, fostering growth in a space filled with love and support.

Foundations of Developmental Therapy at home: Principles to Follow

1. Meeting Your Child Where They Are Every Child's Path is Unique

When Riya first noticed her son Arjun avoiding eye contact, she felt overwhelmed. Where should she begin? Her therapist suggested starting small—something meaningful yet manageable. One day, as Arjun sat spinning a car wheel, Riya gently rolled a ball toward him. To her surprise, he paused and pushed it back. That fleeting moment of shared attention became the foundation for their bond and marked the beginning of his therapy journey.

Start Small and Build Confidence

Therapy works best when it aligns with a child's strengths and challenges. For instance, if a child struggles with social greetings, practicing a simple wave to familiar faces like grandma can lay the groundwork for more confident interactions in public.

Tailored to Individual Needs

One size doesn't fit all in therapy. A 5-year-old with limited verbal skills might thrive with Picture Exchange Communication Systems (PECS), using pictures to communicate basic needs like "want cookie," instead of engaging in structured conversations. On the other hand, a 3-year-old who knows letters but struggles with joint attention might benefit from social play—rolling a ball back and forth instead of focusing on academic tasks.

Why It Matters

Every small victory—whether a wave, a shared smile, or a picture exchange—builds confidence. Therapy at the child's level fosters joy and learning, replacing frustration with moments of connection and growth.

2. Recognizing and Celebrating Every Milestone

When Aarav finally pointed to the cookie jar and uttered "cookie," his mother Meera felt tears well up in her eyes. It was a single word, but to her, it was a thunderous victory. For weeks, they'd worked on pointing and naming objects during snack time, and now, that small yet monumental moment was here. Meera didn't hesitate—she cheered, hugged Aarav, and handed him the cookie, making sure he knew just how proud she was.

Why Small Wins Matter

For children with autism, every milestone—whether it's pointing, naming, or waving—represents hard work and growth. Celebrating these achievements reinforces positive behavior and builds confidence, encouraging them to try again and again. It's not just a step forward; it's a leap toward independence.

3. Making Therapy Part of Everyday Life

Routines are golden opportunities to embed therapy naturally. For Meera, therapy wasn't about hours of drills but weaving lessons into the rhythm of their day.

- **Mealtime Magic**: Aarav practiced naming foods at the table. "Apple," "milk," or even pointing to his favorite plate became moments of learning.

- **Playtime Practice**: Rolling a ball back and forth turned into a game of patience and turn-taking, teaching cooperation through joy.

- **Bedtime Routines**: Tidying toys together before bedtime became a lesson in transitions and responsibility, ending the day on a calm, accomplished note.

These moments transformed therapy into something seamless—and, more importantly, meaningful.

4. Creating a Structured Routine: A Pathway to Confidence

When Riya's son, Vihaan, struggled with tantrums during transitions, she realized that unpredictability was overwhelming him. So, she decided to introduce a daily routine. Each morning started with a cheerful "Good morning!" followed by brushing teeth, breakfast, and getting dressed. Within weeks, Vihaan began anticipating each step, moving from one activity to the next with ease.

Why Routines Matter

For children like Vihaan, routines act as anchors in a sea of unpredictability. Knowing what comes next helps them feel secure, reducing anxiety and creating a calm space for growth. Predictable patterns also help minimize meltdowns, setting the stage for smoother days.

Building Meaningful Routines

- **Morning Magic**: Start the day with consistency—wake up, brush teeth, eat breakfast, and get dressed in the same order. Riya found that labeling each task helped Vihaan feel more in control.

- **Playtime Patterns**: Whether it was sensory play with sand or puzzles at the table, Riya dedicated time for structured play with clear starts and finishes.

- **Bedtime Bliss**: A warm bath, a bedtime story, and a hug became Vihaan's signal that it was time to sleep, promoting better rest and fewer bedtime battles.

Why It's Transformative

Routines aren't just for your child—they bring balance to your entire family. By embedding learning into daily life, you create a world where progress feels natural, achievable, and fun.

Chapter 10

Home Based Developmental Therapy Techniques: Unlocking Communication

When Neha's son, Aarav, turned two, she eagerly waited for him to call her "Mama." But instead of words, Aarav expressed himself through gestures or by leading her to what he wanted. Neha often felt helpless, wondering how to bridge the gap between them. Then, a speech therapist introduced her to developmental therapy techniques that transformed their world.

One afternoon, as Aarav played with his favorite blocks, Neha used a picture card with a block on it. "Aarav, block," she said, holding it up. Aarav looked at the card, then at Neha, and pointed at the block. Neha's heart swelled as she handed it to him, saying, "Yes, block!" This simple exchange was the beginning of their journey toward communication.

Unlocking the Power of Words

Communication is more than speaking—it's about expressing needs, sharing emotions, and building connections. For children like Aarav, developmental therapy opens doors by meeting them where they are and guiding them step by step toward effective expression.

A. Early Intervention for Non-Verbal Children:

For non-verbal children, communication begins with the simplest gestures and symbols, laying the groundwork for their unique voice. Early intervention transforms frustration into connection, as children learn to express their needs in creative ways. With tools like picture cards or sign language, every exchanged look or pointed picture becomes a powerful conversation starter.

1. Picture Exchange Communication System (PECS): Turning Pictures into Voices

Story: Meet Anaya, a 4-year-old who loves cookies but often throws tantrums when she can't get what she wants. Her parents, unsure of her needs, felt helpless until they introduced PECS. One day, Anaya handed her mom a picture of a cookie instead of crying. Her mom was thrilled—Anaya had found her voice through pictures.

How It Works:

- The child is given a picture symbol of an object or activity (like a cookie).

- They hand the picture to an adult to receive the item.

- Over time, they learn to use pictures for various needs like asking for help or a break.

Why It Matters: For children like Anaya, PECS reduces frustration, giving them a reliable way to communicate.

2. Sign Language: Words at Their Fingertips

Story: Rahul, a bright 3-year-old, struggled to say "water" when thirsty, leading to tears and confusion. His mother introduced sign language, teaching him to sign "drink." One day, Rahul signed for water with a big smile, and his mom immediately knew what he wanted.

How It Works:

- Start with simple signs like "more," "please," or "eat."

- Pair the signs with spoken words to build understanding.

- Gradually expand the child's vocabulary as they gain confidence.

Why It Matters: Sign language empowers children like Rahul to express their needs even when words fail.

3. Encouraging Vocalization Through Play: Sounds of Fun

Story: Arya loved her toy animals but rarely made a sound. During a play session, her dad imitated a cow's "moo" and encouraged Arya to do the same. At first, she giggled but soon joined in. Her "moo" became the first step toward vocal communication.

How It Works:

- Play with engaging toys like animals, cars, or dolls, encouraging the child to mimic sounds or simple words.

- Reward attempts at vocalization with praise or smiles, even if the sounds aren't perfect.

- Use repetition to reinforce learning in a playful context.

Why It Matters: Play removes pressure, making vocal practice fun and natural for children like Arya.

Why These Techniques Work

These strategies meet children where they are, using tools tailored to their needs. PECS, sign language, and playful vocalizations give children pathways to express themselves, reducing frustration and opening the door to deeper connections with their families.

For parents, every step—whether it's a simple "moo" or a signed "more"—is a moment to celebrate. Communication is not just about words; it's about understanding, and these techniques ensure your child is heard in their own unique way.

B. Developing Verbal Skills: Unlocking Your Child's Voice

Every word a child speaks is like a precious gem for parents, especially when those words come after consistent effort and loving guidance. For children with Autism Spectrum Disorder (ASD), developing verbal skills often requires patience, creative strategies, and a touch of storytelling to make learning fun. Here's how parents can turn everyday moments into opportunities for speech development.

1. Techniques for Teaching Simple Words and Phrases

Story: Meet Arjun, a 4-year-old fascinated by cars but hesitant to speak. His mom noticed he loved pointing to cars outside the window. One day, she started saying, "Big car," every time he pointed. Slowly, Arjun began mimicking her words, eventually exclaiming, "Big car!" on his own during a drive. It was a breakthrough moment for his family.

How It Works:

- Start with simple, functional phrases like "want juice" or "mommy help."

- Use these phrases during everyday activities to create meaningful connections between words and actions.

- Encourage your child to repeat or attempt the words, praising their efforts warmly.

Why It Matters: By linking words to their immediate needs or interests, children like Arjun feel motivated to speak, turning curiosity into communication.

2. The Power of Repetition and Modeling

Story: At snack time, Maya always pointed at the cookie jar but never said a word. Her dad consistently modeled the phrase, "I want a cookie." At first, Maya would only giggle, but one afternoon, she surprised him by saying, "Cookie!" It wasn't perfect, but it was her first step toward verbalizing her needs.

How It Works:

- Repeat target words or phrases consistently during relevant activities. For example, while building with blocks, say, "Stack block" or "Red block."

- Encourage the child to imitate the words and provide positive reinforcement when they try.

- Celebrate even small attempts, as these build confidence.

Example:

If your child says "car" while pointing, expand their phrase by modeling, "Yes, that's a red car!" This not only reinforces their word but also shows them how to use descriptive language.

Why These Techniques Work

These strategies align speech development with your child's interests and everyday activities, making learning feel natural and enjoyable. For parents, each word or phrase spoken by their child is a small victory, proof of the power of love, patience, and persistence. By teaching through connection and repetition, you're not just building vocabulary—you're opening the door to a lifetime of communication.

C. Using Visual Aids: Unlocking Communication Through Pictures and Symbols

For children with Autism Spectrum Disorder (ASD), visual aids are like a secret language—clear, consistent, and easy to understand. These tools bridge the gap between understanding and expression, making communication and routines feel manageable and predictable. Here's how visual aids can become your child's everyday superheroes.

1. Visual Schedules: Turning Chaos into Clarity

Story: Every morning was a whirlwind for Aditi and her son, Vihaan. He would resist brushing his teeth or getting dressed, overwhelmed by not knowing what was coming next. Then Aditi introduced a visual schedule. A chart with pictures of a toothbrush, breakfast plate, and school bag transformed mornings into a calm, predictable routine. Vihaan began looking forward to moving each picture to the "completed" section—a small but meaningful victory.

How It Works:

a. Use pictures or symbols for each activity, like a bed for "wake up" or a book for "storytime."

b. Arrange them in order to outline the day's routine.

c. Allow your child to move each picture as they complete the task.

Example:

Morning visuals might include:

1. A picture of a bed for "wake up."

2. A toothbrush for "brush teeth."

3. A plate of food for "eat breakfast."

Why It Matters: Visual schedules help children feel in control of their day, reducing anxiety and encouraging independence.

2. Emotion Charts: Expressing the Inexpressible

Story: Little Aarav would burst into tears seemingly out of nowhere. His mom, Maya, couldn't figure out what was wrong. One day, she introduced an emotion chart with colorful faces showing emotions like happy, sad, or angry. When Aarav had a meltdown, Maya gently guided him to the chart. Pointing to the "angry" face, Aarav finally communicated his frustration. This became their go-to method for understanding his feelings.

How It Works:

- Place an emotion chart with faces showing various emotions (e.g., happy, sad, scared) in an accessible spot.

- When the child feels upset, encourage them to point to the face that matches their feelings.

- Use the chart to start a conversation about their emotions and how to cope with them.

Example:

If your child points to "sad," you might say, "I see you're feeling sad. Did something happen?" This can help them feel heard and understood.

Why It Matters: Emotion charts teach children to identify, label, and express their feelings, laying the foundation for emotional regulation.

3. Flashcards: Building Vocabulary, One Picture at a Time

Story: Ananya loved animals but struggled to name them. Her dad used flashcards with pictures of a dog, cat, and bird. He would say, "This is a dog," and encourage her to repeat it. At first, Ananya hesitated, but soon she was proudly pointing and saying, "Dog!" Flashcards became their favorite bonding activity.

How It Works:

- Show your child a flashcard with a picture or word and say it aloud.

- Encourage them to repeat the word or point to the object in their environment.

- Gradually increase complexity by introducing more detailed cards as they improve.

Example:

Use animal flashcards to teach words like "dog," "cat," or "bird." Say the word, and praise the child for repeating or identifying the picture.

Why It Matters: Flashcards are versatile tools that make learning interactive and fun, helping children build vocabulary and understanding at their own pace.

Visual Aids: Your Everyday Superpower

Visual aids aren't just tools—they're bridges into your child's world. Whether it's a schedule that turns chaos into calm, an emotion chart that unlocks feelings, or flashcards that spark new words, these aids help children navigate their day with confidence. For parents, these moments of connection and growth are priceless, turning challenges into opportunities for learning and bonding.

Chapter 11

The Power of Connection: Building Social Skills at Home in Autism

Sonal watched as her son, Aryan, sat in the corner, spinning the wheels of his toy car while the other children played together. "Why doesn't he look up when I call his name?" she wondered, feeling a pang of isolation. Social interactions, which seemed so natural for other children, felt like an insurmountable hurdle for Aryan. Determined to help him connect with the world, Sonal began exploring strategies that could bring him closer to shared experiences, starting with small, meaningful steps.

This is the journey many parents face when teaching social skills to children with Autism Spectrum Disorder (ASD). Social interaction is not just about playdates or conversations; it's about teaching a child the joy of shared experiences, eye contact, and connection. Let's explore how developmental therapy can open doors to a world of meaningful relationships.

Encouraging Joint Attention

Joint attention, the ability to share focus on an object or activity with another person, is the cornerstone of social interaction. For Aryan, this began with something simple: his mother pointing to the spinning car and saying, "Wow, it's going fast!" Slowly, he looked up, first at the car, then at her.

Small steps like these help children engage with others, setting the stage for deeper connections. Joint attention activities, such as pointing at objects, sharing a book, or rolling a ball back and forth, create a foundation for meaningful social relationships.

A. Building Bridges Through Play: Encouraging Social Interaction

When Ananya noticed her son Aarav was always in his own world, she wondered how to bring him closer to hers. One day, while flipping through a picture book, she pointed to a bright yellow bird and said, "Look, Aarav! What a big bird!" To her surprise, Aarav glanced at the page, his eyes following her finger. That fleeting moment was a breakthrough—a first step toward shared experiences.

Encouraging joint attention like this helps children with autism connect with others by focusing on the same object or activity. It's a simple yet powerful way to foster interaction.

1. Activities Like Pointing at Objects Together or Shared Play

How to Practice:

- Sit with your child and choose something engaging, like a shiny toy or colorful picture.

- Point to the object and say, "Look, it's a ball!" Encourage them to follow your gaze.

- Celebrate any response—whether it's a glance, a sound, or pointing back—with a big smile or gentle praise.

Example:

While reading a book together, point to a blue butterfly and say, "Do you see the butterfly?" Over time, these shared moments teach your child to focus on what you're showing them, strengthening your bond.

2. Using Games to Promote Turn-Taking

One evening, Ananya introduced a simple ball-rolling game to Aarav. "Here comes the ball!" she said as she gently rolled it to him. At first, Aarav just watched it stop at his feet. But after a few tries, he hesitantly rolled it back. "Your turn!" she cheered, clapping her hands. Aarav's small action was a big victory.

How to Practice:

- Play easy games like rolling a ball, building with blocks, or a basic puzzle.

- Use clear phrases like, "It's my turn," and "Now it's your turn."

- Be patient and praise their effort every time they wait or take their turn.

Example:

While stacking blocks, encourage them to wait for their turn to add a piece. Say, "Now it's your turn!" as you pass them the block, reinforcing patience and cooperation.

Why It Matters:

These simple activities do more than entertain—they teach children the building blocks of interaction, from shared attention to cooperative play. Each small step helps prepare them for deeper social connections and meaningful relationships.

B. Helping Children Build Friendships: Developing Peer Interaction

When Aarush joined his first playdate, his mother, Meera, watched nervously from the sidelines. Aarush loved stacking blocks at home but had never played with other children. As the other kids started building a block tower, Aarush hesitated. Meera gently guided him, whispering, "Ask for the red block." Slowly, Aarush pointed and said, "Red block, please." The other child handed it over with a smile. Aarush added the block to the tower, and Meera's heart swelled. It was a small moment, but a huge step toward connecting with peers.

1. Structured Playdates and Group Activities

Structured playdates provide a safe, controlled environment for children with autism to learn social interaction.

How to Practice:

- Invite one or two children for a playdate in a familiar setting, like your home.

- Choose simple activities with clear roles—building blocks, completing puzzles, or playing pretend.

- Stay nearby to gently guide interactions, prompting your child to share or take turns.

Example:

During a block-building activity, guide your child to ask, "Can I have the blue block?" When it's another child's turn, encourage them to wait and say, "Your turn now!"

Tips for Success:

- Keep the playdates short at first and gradually increase their duration as your child gains confidence.

- Celebrate small victories, like sharing a toy or exchanging smiles, to reinforce positive experiences.

2. Teaching Social Cues Through Role-Play

Role-playing transforms abstract social concepts into relatable, tangible experiences.

How to Practice:

- Use puppets, dolls, or toys to act out common social situations, such as greeting a friend, asking for help, or sharing.

- Model both appropriate and inappropriate behaviors, then discuss the difference.

Example:

Act out a scenario where one puppet asks another, "Can I have your toy?" The second puppet responds, "Yes, let's play together!" Encourage your child to try the dialogue themselves, practicing in a safe, low-pressure setting.

Why It Matters:

For children with autism, structured activities and role-playing provide essential practice for navigating social situations. Each small interaction—whether asking for a toy or smiling at a peer—builds a foundation for friendships, empathy, and understanding. As they gain these skills, children can connect more confidently with the world around them.

Building Bridges: Why Social Interaction Skills Matter

Imagine a world where a simple smile, a shared glance, or a playful "your turn" becomes a gateway to connection. For children with Autism Spectrum Disorder (ASD), developing social interaction skills is not just about learning to participate—it's about opening doors to friendships, building confidence, and finding joy in shared experiences. By fostering these skills through targeted techniques like joint attention, turn-taking, structured play, and role-playing, parents and caregivers can empower children to thrive in social settings.

Practical Tips for Parents: Turning Small Steps into Big Progress

1. **Start Small**

   Think of social interactions as stepping stones. Begin with one-on-one activities like rolling a ball back and forth with your child. Once they're comfortable, gradually introduce small group settings where they can practice with others.

2. **Celebrate the Wins**

   Every effort is a victory. When your child waits their turn in a game or smiles at a peer, celebrate with a cheerful "Well done!" or a high-five. Positive reinforcement fuels their confidence and encourages them to keep trying.

3. **Be Patient**

   Rome wasn't built in a day, and neither are social skills. Progress may come in tiny increments, but each step forward is a foundation for the next. Focus on the journey, not the timeline.

4. **Tap Into Their Interests**

   Does your child love trains, dolls, or dinosaurs? Use their favorite toys to create opportunities for interaction. For example, have them share a dinosaur figure during play or take turns building a train track with a friend.

With consistency, patience, and encouragement, parents can weave social skills development into everyday routines, making it both natural and enjoyable. Over time, these efforts will help children with autism feel not just included but valued, giving them the tools to connect with others and participate meaningfully in their communities. Every shared smile and exchanged word is a step toward a brighter, more connected future.

Chapter 12

Small Steps, Big Leaps: Developing Motor Skills at Home in Children with Autism

The playground was bustling with laughter and energy, but little Rohan stood at the edge, clutching his mother's hand. He wanted to climb the slide and join the fun, but balancing on the ladder felt like a mountain too steep to conquer. "It's okay, Rohan," his mom said gently, kneeling beside him. "Let's take it one step at a time." With her encouragement, he placed one shaky foot on the ladder, then another. By the end of the day, Rohan was sliding down with a triumphant smile, waving at his mother every time he reached the bottom.

For children with Autism Spectrum Disorder (ASD), motor skill challenges often mean missing out on such moments of joy. These skills—both fine, like buttoning a shirt, and gross, like jumping or running—are essential for independence, social interaction, and confidence. Through developmental therapy, parents and caregivers can help children like Rohan gain the strength, coordination, and courage to explore their world, one small step at a time.

This chapter dives into practical, engaging strategies to nurture fine and gross motor skills, transforming everyday activities into opportunities for growth. From threading beads to building obstacle courses, let's explore how families can make motor skill development a natural and joyful part of their child's life.

A. Building Confidence, One Tiny Movement at a Time: Fine Motor Skills Development

Fine motor skills are like the brushstrokes of independence. Whether it's zipping a jacket, writing their name, or picking up a spoon, these small tasks help children with Autism Spectrum Disorder (ASD) navigate their world with confidence. Let's dive into activities that make strengthening these skills a joyful experience.

1. Threading Beads: Building Dexterity Through Play

When six-year-old Tara saw her mom lay out a rainbow of beads and a sturdy string, her eyes lit up. "We're making jewelry!" her mom exclaimed. At first, Tara struggled to pick up the larger beads, fumbling with her fingers. But with encouragement and a bit of patience, she proudly threaded a bright red bead onto the string. "Let's make a pattern!" her mom suggested, introducing an extra layer of fun.

How to Practice:

- Use large, colorful beads for beginners and introduce smaller beads as skills improve.

- Create patterns (e.g., red-blue-red) to engage their attention and add a cognitive challenge.

Why It's Fun: Tara not only improved her hand-eye coordination but also beamed with pride wearing her self-made necklace.

2. Drawing and Coloring: The Art of Fine Motor Growth

Amir loved watching his older brother draw rockets and dinosaurs. "Can I try?" he asked one day. Equipped with jumbo crayons, Amir started with scribbles but soon graduated to tracing dotted lines his mom prepared. "It's a spaceship!" he declared, holding up his creation.

How to Practice:

- Offer easy-to-grip crayons or markers for younger kids.

- Encourage tracing shapes like circles and squares before advancing to animals or vehicles.

Why It's Fun: Amir's scribbles became masterpieces, building finger strength and inspiring his creativity.

3. Building with Blocks: From Towers to Masterpieces

Three-year-old Nikhil loved knocking over block towers his dad built. "How about we build one together?" his dad suggested.

Slowly, Nikhil began stacking blocks himself, giggling each time a tower stood tall.

How to Practice:

- Start with simple towers and encourage more complex designs, like houses or bridges.

- Use interlocking blocks like LEGO for added challenges.

Why It's Fun: Nikhil didn't just develop his fine motor skills—he learned teamwork and problem-solving too.

Why These Moments Matter

Every bead threaded, shape traced, and block stacked is more than an activity—it's a step toward independence. These joyful moments teach children that small achievements lead to big wins, building their confidence and unlocking new possibilities.

B. Leaping Forward: Gross Motor Skills Development

Developing gross motor skills is like giving a child the keys to explore their world. These big muscle movements—walking, jumping, or throwing—aren't just fun; they build strength, coordination, and confidence. Here's how you can turn these skills into joyful adventures at home.

1. Jumping Activities: Bouncing into Confidence

When five-year-old Aarav saw the hopscotch grid his mom drew on the patio, he hesitated. "Just jump to the yellow square," she encouraged. Aarav gave it a shot, landing clumsily at first, but his giggles grew with each leap. Soon, he was calling out colors and hopping with newfound confidence.

How to Practice:

- Begin with simple jumping in place or hopping on one foot.

- Turn it into a game: Create a hopscotch grid with chalk or tape on the floor.

- Supervised trampoline sessions add an extra layer of fun and sensory input.

Why It's Fun: Aarav didn't just improve his balance and strength—his joyful jumps became a bonding moment with his mom.

2. Throwing and Catching: Small Tosses, Big Wins

Four-year-old Mia had never caught a ball before, so her dad started with a balloon. "Here it comes!" he said, tossing it gently. Mia squealed as she caught it with both hands. A week later, she was tossing a soft foam ball back with confidence, her grin growing wider with each catch.

How to Practice:

- Start with lightweight, slow-moving objects like balloons or foam balls.

- Roll a ball on the ground to introduce the motion before moving to tossing and catching.

- Gradually increase the distance as skills improve.

Why It's Fun: Mia's delight in her growing coordination made playtime a highlight of the day for her and her dad.

3. Obstacle Courses: Adventures in Movement

Seven-year-old Raj loved crawling through "forts," so his mom turned their living room into an adventure course. "Jump over the pillow, crawl under the chair, and balance on the taped line!" she instructed. Raj completed it with gusto, asking, "Can we do it again?"

How to Practice:

- Use cushions for jumping over, chairs for crawling under, and tape to create balancing lines.

- Guide your child step-by-step, adding a timer for an extra challenge.

- Encourage problem-solving by letting them decide how to navigate obstacles.

Why It's Fun: Raj's obstacle course wasn't just exercise—it was an imaginative journey through a "forest" filled with challenges he couldn't wait to conquer.

Why It Matters

Gross motor activities aren't just about movement—they're about building the foundation for independence and confidence. Whether it's jumping, throwing, or navigating an obstacle course, these small adventures empower children to engage in the world around them, preparing them for playground fun, sports, and so much more.

Tips for Parents and Caregivers: Turning Growth into Joy

Parenting a child with autism is a journey filled with both challenges and unique joys. Here are practical tips, sprinkled with relatable stories, to help you make the most of developmental activities at home.

1. Make It Fun: Transforming Therapy into Play

When six-year-old Zara refused to join her therapy session, her mom got creative. "Let's hop like bunnies to the carrot patch!" she exclaimed. Zara's giggles filled the room as she jumped from mat to mat, unaware she was practicing balance and coordination.

Tip: Choose activities that reflect your child's interests. Love animals? Try "slithering like a snake" for core strength or "flapping like a bird" to encourage arm movements. Turning exercises into a playful adventure keeps your child engaged and excited to participate.

2. Be Patient: Celebrate Small Steps

It took weeks for three-year-old Kian to grasp the concept of rolling a ball back and forth. But the day he did, his parents cheered as though he'd scored a goal. Kian's smile said it all—he felt proud of his achievement.

Tip: Progress might come slowly, but every small win is a milestone worth celebrating. Whether it's a new word, a better balance, or simply an attempt, let your child know how proud you are. Your encouragement will keep them motivated.

3. Create a Safe Environment: Comfort Fuels Confidence

Five-year-old Arya was hesitant to try jumping exercises until her dad laid down foam mats and cleared the living room of sharp-edged furniture. "Now it's your turn!" he said, as Arya gleefully leaped onto the soft mats, laughing with each attempt.

Tip: Ensure the area is hazard-free, with soft surfaces like foam mats or cushions. A safe space lets your child focus on exploring movements without fear of injury.

4. Incorporate Into Daily Routines: Lessons in Everyday Moments

Sahil loved grocery shopping with his mom. She handed him a small bag of apples to carry, turning the trip into a motor skills exercise. "You're so strong!" she said, as he beamed with pride.

Tip: Sneak practice into everyday activities. Let your child zip up their jacket, squeeze toothpaste onto their toothbrush, or carry lightweight items. These small tasks encourage fine and gross motor development seamlessly.

5. Adapt to Your Child's Needs: Flexibility Wins

Four-year-old Nia struggled with threading beads, so her therapist started with larger, brightly colored ones. As Nia's coordination improved, she moved on to smaller beads, gaining confidence with each success.

Tip: Tailor activities to your child's current abilities. Start simple, and as they master each step, gradually introduce more complexity. Flexibility ensures that your child feels capable and avoids frustration.

By weaving patience, creativity, and adaptability into your daily routines, you're not just a caregiver—you're a coach, cheerleader, and partner in your child's growth. Every hop, every attempt, and every smile brings you both closer to triumphs big and small.

Chapter 13

Behavioral Support at Home: Turning Challenges into Opportunities

On a sunny afternoon, Meera watched her son Aarav build a block tower, his favorite activity. Suddenly, the loud crash of a falling toy startled him. Within seconds, his joy turned into distress.

Aarav threw himself on the floor, wailing inconsolably. Meera felt a familiar wave of helplessness. Was this another tantrum, or something deeper?

For parents like Meera, navigating behavioral challenges can feel like walking a tightrope. Behaviors like meltdowns, rigidity, or resistance to change are not acts of defiance but expressions of deeper discomfort. Developmental therapy offers a way to decode these behaviors, turning them into opportunities for connection and growth.

Behavioral support is not about fixing or controlling—it's about understanding and responding with compassion. In this chapter, we'll explore how parents can address meltdowns, create calming strategies, and reinforce positive behaviors, transforming daily challenges into moments of progress.

Just like Meera learned to recognize Aarav's sensory triggers and create a calm space for him to recover, you too can discover ways to better understand your child's unique needs. Let's begin the journey of turning behavioral hurdles into stepping stones for growth and trust.

Understanding Triggers and Calming Strategies: Helping Your Child Find Balance

1. Identifying Triggers and Managing Sensory Overload

Every Saturday morning, Aditi and her daughter Anya went to the grocery store. What started as a happy outing often turned into a battle. The bustling crowd, harsh fluorescent lights, and loud music overwhelmed Anya, leading to meltdowns in the middle of the aisle. Aditi realized this wasn't about defiance—it was sensory overload.

How to Identify Triggers:

Start by observing your child closely. What happens just before a meltdown? Anya's distress always began when they reached the loudspeaker near the produce section. Aditi kept a log and identified other patterns, like her daughter's struggles with sudden changes in routine.

Managing Sensory Overload:

Once Aditi recognized the triggers, she packed noise-canceling headphones and sunglasses for grocery trips. She also created a quiet corner at home with a soft beanbag, a favorite stuffed animal, and a weighted blanket to help Anya decompress.

Example:

If your child reacts to bright lights or loud noises, sensory tools can help. Like Aditi, use sunglasses, headphones, or a small fidget toy to provide comfort and control.

2. Calming Techniques: Building Emotional Resilience

One evening, Aarav was upset after losing a game. He clenched his fists, tears streaming down his face. His mother, Priya, knelt beside him with a pinwheel. "Blow the wheel," she said gently.

Aarav's focused breaths slowed his sobs, and he began to calm down.

Breathing Exercises:

Deep breaths work wonders. Introduce visual aids like bubbles or pinwheels to make the practice engaging. Aarav loved watching the pinwheel spin, which turned a stressful moment into a calming exercise.

Using a Sensory Corner:

Priya also created a sensory corner for Aarav. Whenever he felt overwhelmed, she gently guided him to the corner where a soft rug, stress balls, and dim lighting helped him relax. It became his personal refuge.

Example:

If your child struggles with transitions, introduce a sensory corner as a safe space. It's not just a physical area—it's an emotional sanctuary.

Why It Matters

By identifying triggers and using calming strategies, parents like Aditi and Priya have transformed moments of distress into opportunities for connection and growth. These tools teach children to manage their emotions, leading to fewer and less intense meltdowns over time.

Reinforcement Strategies: Building Positive Behaviors Through Encouragement

1. Positive Reinforcement for Desired Behaviors

When four-year-old Ria handed her father a picture card of a cookie instead of crying, he smiled and said, "Great job asking for a cookie!" He immediately handed her the treat. Ria's smile lit up the room as she realized her efforts were rewarded.

How It Works:

Positive reinforcement turns everyday moments into celebrations of progress. Identify the behavior you want to encourage—like using words to ask for something or sharing toys. Reward the action right away to strengthen the connection between the behavior and the reward.

Examples:

- **Communication:** If a child uses a picture card to request water, respond enthusiastically, "You did such a great job asking for water!" and give them the water immediately.

- **Sharing:** When a child shares a toy with their sibling, say, "That was very kind of you!" and perhaps let them pick the next activity.

Tips for Success:

- Be consistent, especially when introducing new behaviors.

- Keep rewards simple and immediate, such as a high-five, a favorite snack, or a short break for play.

2. Using Token Systems: Teaching Patience and Planning

Seven-year-old Aarav was reluctant to brush his teeth. His mother introduced a star chart, where he earned a star for each completed chore. After five stars, he could choose a reward—baking cookies with her or an extra 10 minutes of screen time. Aarav's excitement to earn stars transformed his routine into a game.

How It Works:

Token systems teach delayed gratification. Assign tokens, stickers, or stars for specific behaviors like brushing teeth or completing homework. Once a child earns a set number of tokens, let them exchange them for a bigger reward.

Example:

If a child earns a sticker for every chore they complete, they could exchange five stickers for a trip to the park or a small toy.

Why It Matters:

Token systems teach children to connect effort with results, fostering a sense of responsibility and achievement.

Positive reinforcement and token systems give children the motivation to embrace desirable behaviors. By celebrating small victories, parents create a nurturing environment where children feel proud of their achievements and are eager to continue improving. Whether it's a high-five, a sticker, or a fun activity, every reward brings them closer to mastering new skills with confidence.

Practical Tips for Parents: Navigating Challenges with Calm and Confidence

Parenting a child with autism can be filled with rewarding milestones and challenging moments. Here are actionable tips to help you navigate with grace and empathy:

1. Stay Calm and Consistent: Leading by Example

When six-year-old Maya had a meltdown over a broken toy, her mother took a deep breath, knelt to Maya's level, and said gently, "Let's take a break and figure this out together." Maya began to calm down, mirroring her mom's steady demeanor.

Why It Matters:

Children pick up on their caregiver's emotions. Remaining calm can help de-escalate tense situations and create a sense of security.

2. Use Clear and Simple Language: Keep It Straightforward

When Aarav struggled to tidy his toys, his father said, "Put the blocks in the box," instead of giving multiple instructions. Aarav completed the task and smiled at the praise: "Great job putting your toys away!"

Tip:

Short, specific phrases make it easier for children to understand expectations and feel accomplished.

3. Be Patient: Progress Happens One Step at a Time

Meera celebrated when her son, who previously avoided eye contact, made brief eye contact during a game. While it seemed small, it was a huge win in their journey.

Why It Matters:

Behavioral changes take time. Focus on small victories and build from there.

4. Set Realistic Expectations: Tailoring Goals to Your Child

When Rohan's therapist suggested teaching gestures before verbal requests, his parents embraced the idea. They realized setting achievable steps helped Rohan communicate without frustration.

Tip:

Understand your child's developmental level and break goals into manageable steps. Success is more likely when challenges feel attainable.

5. Involve the Child: Empower Them to Take Charge

When Priya noticed her daughter getting overwhelmed, she guided her to their sensory corner and let her choose a calming item. Priya's daughter picked a squishy toy, taking comfort in the decision.

Why It Matters:

Teaching children to recognize their triggers and choose strategies they enjoy fosters independence and emotional regulation.

These tips empower parents to nurture growth with patience and understanding, turning daily challenges into opportunities for connection and progress.

Chapter 14

Steering Sensory Overload: Finding Balance Through Tailored Activities

When Excitement Turns to Overwhelm

Ravi's eyes sparkled as his family entered the bustling mall. The colorful displays and cheerful chatter filled him with excitement. But soon, the joy faded. The hum of voices grew louder, the lights became too bright, and the endless motion of the crowd felt like chaos. Clutching his mom's hand, Ravi covered his ears and began to sob. A fun outing had turned into a storm of panic.

For Ravi's parents, this was another reminder of how uniquely he experienced the world. They wondered: *How can we make him feel safe? How can we help him thrive in environments that feel so overwhelming?*

This is the journey many parents of children with Autism Spectrum Disorder (ASD) embark on. Sensory activities, thoughtfully tailored to each child, can turn moments of distress into opportunities for comfort, focus, and growth. They unlock a world where every child feels understood.

The Unique Sensory World of Each Child

Every child with ASD interacts with sensory input differently, much like each has a unique personality. For some, the world is too loud, bright, or busy. For others, it's too quiet, dull, or still.

- **Hyper-sensitive children**, like Mira, may shrink from loud sounds or uncomfortable textures, wincing at a vacuum cleaner's whir or refusing to wear certain fabrics.

- **Hypo-sensitive children**, like Arya, crave sensory stimulation, spinning in circles, seeking hugs, or bouncing off furniture to feel engaged.

With the right sensory activities, children like Ravi, Mira, and Arya can discover balance in their worlds. These activities not only soothe or stimulate their senses but also empower them to navigate life's complexities with greater ease.

Understanding Hyper- and Hypo-Sensitivity: A Journey into Your Child's Sensory World

Every parent of a child with Autism Spectrum Disorder (ASD) knows the challenge of decoding their child's unique sensory needs. Through thoughtful observation and tailored activities, these sensory differences can be understood and supported, creating a more balanced world for your child.

Hyper-Sensitivity: When the World Feels Too Loud

Riya's Story: Riya's family was excited about a backyard barbecue. But as soon as the grill was lit and the neighbours' music started, Riya ran inside, hands clamped over her ears. The sizzle of the grill, the chatter of guests, and the distant bass of music were too much for her. She curled up in her favorite chair, refusing to return outside.

Understanding Hyper-Sensitivity:

For children like Riya, the world can feel overwhelming. Sounds, textures, or lights that seem ordinary to others may feel unbearable.

Common Triggers:

- **Sounds:** A vacuum's roar or a bustling crowd might send a child running for quiet.

- **Textures:** Certain clothes or food textures may make them pull away.

- **Lights:** Bright or flickering lights can cause avoidance or distress.

Signs to Watch For:

- Covering ears or shutting eyes.

- Avoiding touch or specific places.

- Meltdowns triggered by sensory overload.

Small Changes, Big Differences:

Riya's parents now offer noise-canceling headphones during noisy events and choose soft, breathable fabrics for her clothes, ensuring her comfort.

Hypo-Sensitivity: When the World Feels Too Quiet

Aryan's Story:

Aryan was always on the move—spinning in circles, crashing onto the sofa, and humming loudly as he played. His parents noticed that he often pressed his hands against the walls or squeezed objects tightly, seeking sensations that grounded him.

Understanding Hypo-Sensitivity:

For children like Aryan, the world might not provide enough stimulation, prompting them to seek sensory input.

Common Behaviors:

- **Movement:** Spinning, jumping, or running gives them the stimulation they crave.

- **Touch:** Strong hugs or rough textures feel satisfying.

- **Sounds:** They may hum or prefer environments with steady background noise.

Signs to Watch For:

- Seeking pressure or physical sensations.

- Minimal reaction to pain, sound, or temperature changes.

- Repetitive movements like bouncing or spinning.

Engaging Their Senses:

Aryan's parents introduced a mini trampoline and tactile play with kinetic sand, channeling his sensory needs into constructive and enjoyable activities.

Why Understanding Matters

By recognizing whether your child experiences hyper- or hypo-sensitivity, you can tailor environments and activities to meet their needs. Whether it's creating a quiet sensory corner or providing stimulating toys, these adjustments empower children to engage with the world more comfortably and confidently.

Tailored Sensory Activities: Balancing Calm and Energy

Every child with Autism Spectrum Disorder (ASD) experiences the world differently, and their sensory needs reflect that uniqueness. For some, the challenge is finding calm in overwhelming environments, while others crave stimulation to stay engaged. Tailored sensory activities are like a personalized toolkit, helping children regulate their emotions and connect with the world around them.

1. Calming Techniques: Finding Comfort in Chaos

Maya's Quiet Escape:

Maya, a 5-year-old, struggled with noisy playdates. After an hour of games, she'd retreat to her room, overwhelmed and anxious. Her parents noticed the change and introduced a weighted blanket during her downtime. Wrapped in its soft embrace, Maya's breathing slowed, and her fidgeting ceased. Now, playdates end with her reading under her blanket—a moment of calm amidst the chaos.

Examples of Calming Techniques:

- **Weighted Blankets:** Provide deep pressure, helping children feel grounded. Perfect for quiet moments like bedtime or storytime.

- **Soft Music:** Gentle sounds like ocean waves or lullabies can ease auditory sensitivities. A soft playlist transformed Maya's meltdowns into peaceful reflections.

- **Sensory Corners:** A small space with dim lighting, plush pillows, and favorite toys offers a safe retreat. After school, Maya's corner became her favorite spot to decompress.

2. Stimulating Techniques: Energizing Engagement

Aarav's Bounce to Focus:

Aarav, 6, couldn't sit still during homework time. He'd fidget, hum, and lose track of his tasks. His parents added a trampoline to his daily routine. Aarav now jumps for 10 minutes before homework. The rhythmic motion energizes him while also channeling his restlessness, transforming study time into productive moments.

Examples of Stimulating Techniques:

- **Tactile Activities:** Playdough and kinetic sand provide endless opportunities for exploration. Aarav loves sculpting imaginary creatures, improving both his focus and creativity.

- **Swinging:** A hammock in the backyard became his go-to after school, offering balance and motion that calmed his energy.

- **Jumping and Bouncing:** A therapy ball in the living room turned transitions into fun. Aarav happily bounces before dinner, releasing pent-up energy.

Why These Activities Matter

Children like Maya and Aarav thrive when their sensory needs are met with thoughtful, personalized activities. Whether it's a quiet moment under a weighted blanket or the joy of tactile play, these techniques foster self-regulation, focus, and confidence, making the world feel just a little more manageable for every child.

Creating a Sensory-Friendly Environment: A World Designed for Comfort

Building a sensory-friendly environment is like creating a sanctuary where children with Autism Spectrum Disorder (ASD) can thrive. Every small adjustment caters to their unique sensory needs, empowering them to navigate daily challenges with confidence.

1. Observe and Adapt: Learning Their Language

Lila's Light-Sensitive World:

Seven-year-old Lila would squint and shy away whenever the overhead lights were turned on. Her parents noticed this and replaced the harsh bulbs with dimmable lamps that emitted a soft glow. Instantly, her playroom became a haven. She now spends hours happily building puzzles, her discomfort a thing of the past.

Key Tip: Watch how your child reacts to different sensory inputs. If bright lights or loud sounds overwhelm them, opt for softer lighting or noise-canceling tools. Adaptations don't just reduce stress—they create opportunities for growth.

2. Offer Choices: Empowering Independence

Ravi's Decision Time:

Ravi loved sensory bins filled with beans but also found solace in calming music. When his mom let him choose between playing with the bin or listening to his favorite nature sounds, Ravi felt in control. He alternated between the two, learning to self-regulate while having fun.

Key Tip: Giving children a say in their sensory activities boosts their engagement and confidence. Offering choices fosters autonomy and ensures they enjoy the experience.

3. Use Visual Supports: Clear and Simple Communication

Maya's Morning Routine:

Maya struggled to understand when and how to use her sensory tools. Her dad created a visual schedule with symbols for activities like swinging, sensory bins, and using her weighted blanket. Each morning, Maya pointed to her choices, eagerly starting her day with structure and clarity.

Key Tip: Use pictures, charts, or symbols to help your child navigate their sensory options. A visual guide transforms confusion into excitement and readiness.

The Power of Sensory Activities: Unlocking Growth and Confidence

Every parent dreams of seeing their child thrive—calm, focused, and confident. For children with Autism Spectrum Disorder (ASD), sensory activities can be the bridge to that dream. By embracing sensory play and tailored interventions, parents can transform overwhelming moments into opportunities for joy and growth.

The Benefits of Sensory Activities

1. Improved Self-Regulation:

Meet Noah, who struggled with meltdowns when overwhelmed. A calming sensory corner with a weighted blanket became his refuge, helping him regain control during stressful moments. Sensory activities like this teach children how to manage emotions and navigate challenges.

2. Enhanced Focus:

Ella used to fidget constantly during homework. Swinging for five minutes before starting helped her feel centered and ready to concentrate. Sensory input, like swinging or tactile play, primes the brain for learning by creating a sense of balance.

3. Better Motor Skills:

Building with kinetic sand helped Liam strengthen his fine motor skills while having fun. Activities like tactile play or jumping on a trampoline enhance both fine and gross motor development, supporting independence in daily tasks.

4. Increased Confidence:

When Maya was given a choice between sensory bins and calming music, she lit up with excitement. Tailored activities empowered her to take control of her sensory experiences, boosting her confidence in making decisions.

Practical Tips for Parents

1. Start Small:

Dip your toes into sensory play with a single activity. Begin with a sensory bin of rice or beans, then gradually introduce new textures like sand or water beads. Observe how your child responds, letting their reactions guide you.

2. Incorporate Activities Into Daily Routines:

Sensory activities aren't just for playtime—they can ease transitions and soothe tricky moments. For instance, encourage your child to swing for a few minutes before homework or use a weighted lap pad during mealtime.

3. Be Flexible:

As your child grows, so will their preferences. If they outgrow playdough, introduce more advanced tactile activities like model-building or clay sculpting.

Why Sensory Activities Matter

Understanding sensory needs unlocks a world of potential for children with autism. Tailored activities reduce stress, enhance focus, and foster independence, turning challenges into achievements. Parents and caregivers who incorporate these strategies into daily life create a nurturing environment where growth feels natural and fun.

Through patience, creativity, and love, sensory activities become not just tools but pathways to a brighter, more confident future.

Chapter 15

Growing Together: Tailoring Guidance to Each Stage of Development

Three-year-old Aanya was fascinated by the way sunlight danced on the floor. She would sit for hours, lost in its patterns, while her peers at daycare chattered and played in groups. Her mother, Priya, was both awed by Aanya's curiosity and concerned about her limited engagement with others. When Aanya's diagnosis of Autism Spectrum Disorder (ASD) came, Priya's first question to the therapist was, "What should I do now? How do I help her grow?"

Across town, Rohan, a ten-year-old with ASD, loved talking about his favorite topics—dinosaurs and outer space. While he could name every type of Tyrannosaurus Rex, he struggled with back-and-forth conversations, often monopolizing discussions. His father wondered how to encourage meaningful connections with friends while nurturing Rohan's unique strengths.

These stories highlight a truth familiar to many parents: every child with ASD follows their own developmental path, shaped by their age and individual abilities. Supporting their growth requires understanding where they are now and meeting them with guidance tailored to their stage of development.

Why Age and Developmental Level Matter

Childhood, especially the early years, is a time of rapid brain development. For children with ASD, age-appropriate activities can make all the difference, helping to build essential skills in communication, social interaction, and motor coordination. Whether it's fostering shared play in a toddler or refining conversation skills in a preteen, targeted strategies unlock opportunities for growth, one step at a time.

The following sections offer guidance for creating age-appropriate interventions, ensuring every moment becomes a stepping stone on their journey. For Priya, Rohan's father, and many others, this approach transforms uncertainty into a clear, actionable plan for nurturing their child's unique potential.

Discovering the World: Supporting Infants and Toddlers (0–3 Years)

When Ayaan, a curious two-year-old, dipped his fingers into a bowl of rice during sensory play, his mother, Leela, watched with delight. For a moment, the textures held his full attention. Then he squealed in joy, scooping the rice into a tiny cup with surprising precision. It was a small but meaningful breakthrough—a step toward building focus and exploring the world around him.

For infants and toddlers with Autism Spectrum Disorder (ASD), early developmental therapy revolves around similar magical moments. Sensory exploration, playful social interactions, and early communication activities create opportunities for growth during this crucial stage.

1. Sensory Exploration: A World at Their Fingertips

Sensory play not only engages a child's curiosity but also helps develop neural connections. Children with autism often have sensory preferences, and these activities can gently expand their comfort zones.

Story: Sensory Bins Bring Calm

Ayaan loved exploring textures. One day, Leela filled a shallow bin with colorful pasta and small toys. As Ayaan sorted the toys, she described the feeling: "Soft pasta, smooth car." His focus shifted from chaotic to calm, as each scoop became an adventure in discovery.

Try This:

- Fill a bin with rice or beans and add scoops or small toys for exploration. Describe textures to build vocabulary: "Rough sponge, cool water."

- Use textured items like bubble wrap or playdough for hands-on fun. Encourage squishing, popping, or molding.

2. Simple Social Interactions: Play as Connection

Social games help toddlers build joint attention and recognize social cues, all through laughter and fun.

Story: The Power of Peek-a-Boo

Whenever Leela played peek-a-boo with Ayaan, his giggles filled the room. Initially hesitant to look her in the eyes, he began anticipating her "boo!" Soon, he started lifting her hands, eager for the next round.

Try This:

- Play peek-a-boo or sing clapping rhymes like "Pat-a-Cake" to engage your toddler. Sit face-to-face, guide their hands if needed, and celebrate every smile or clap.

3. Early Communication: Laying the Foundation

Early communication doesn't always involve words. Gestures, babbling, and mimicry pave the way for verbal skills.

Story: Songs That Spark Interaction

Ayaan loved "The Wheels on the Bus." Leela exaggerated each motion—rolling her hands, beeping her nose for the horn. One day, she paused mid-song, and Ayaan filled the gap with an enthusiastic "beep-beep!"

Try This:

- Sing nursery rhymes with actions, pausing to let your child complete a motion or sound.

- Mimic your child's gestures or babbling to encourage turn-taking. Wave at them, and cheer when they wave back.

By weaving sensory play, social games, and early communication into daily routines, parents like Leela turn everyday moments into milestones. With each scoop of rice, peek-a-boo giggle, and "beep-beep," children with ASD find joy and connection, building a foundation for lifelong growth.

Creating a Nurturing Space for Growth: Turning Everyday Moments Into Learning

When little Aarav sat in his bathtub surrounded by his floating toys, his mom, Meera, seized the opportunity for playful learning. "Where's the duck?" she asked, holding up the bright yellow toy. Aarav giggled and splashed the water. "Duck!" he mimicked, and Meera's heart swelled with pride. It wasn't just bath time—it was a small step in his developmental journey.

For children in their early years, learning happens best when it feels like play. By embedding simple yet powerful activities into daily routines, parents and caregivers can create a supportive environment that encourages growth in communication, social interaction, and motor skills.

1. Make It Playful and Interactive

Children thrive when learning feels fun and natural. Turn everyday moments into opportunities for discovery and joy.

Story: Bath Time Magic

Every evening, Aarav eagerly awaited bath time. As Meera named the toys—"boat," "fish," "duck"—he splashed and repeated the words. What started as a fun game soon became a ritual where Aarav's vocabulary grew, one word at a time.

Try This:

- During bath time, introduce new words by naming toys or describing actions like "splash" and "float."

- Use playtime to practice turn-taking with simple games like rolling a ball back and forth.

2. Use Repetition and Routine

Repetition builds confidence and reinforces learning. Simple, predictable routines help children feel secure while encouraging consistent engagement.

Story: The Greeting Song

Every morning, Meera and Aarav sang the same song: "Good morning, Aarav! How are you today?" At first, he just listened. Over time, he began to clap along, then babble, and eventually echo the greeting with a joyful "Hello!"

Try This:

- Begin mornings with sensory activities like playing with textured toys or blocks, followed by social routines like a song or storytime.

- Repeat simple games like peek-a-boo daily to encourage anticipation and engagement.

3. Focus on Engagement, Not Perfection

Learning is about connection, not outcomes. Celebrate every effort, whether it's a smile, a sound, or a glance.

Story: Celebrating Small Wins

One afternoon, Meera clapped her hands and said, "Your turn!" Aarav didn't mimic her clap but smiled and reached for her hands. Instead of pushing for perfection, Meera celebrated his attempt with a big cheer, and Aarav lit up with excitement.

Try This:

- Encourage interaction without pressuring your child for a specific response.

- Celebrate their unique ways of engaging, like a glance, a laugh, or a gesture, to build confidence and joy.

Why This Matters

The first three years of life are a magical window for building foundational skills in communication, social interaction, and sensory processing. Everyday moments—whether it's bath time, mealtime, or playtime—are golden opportunities for growth.

By making learning playful, consistent, and pressure-free, parents like Meera empower their children to explore the world with confidence. It's not about perfection; it's about celebrating the journey, one splash, one song, and one smile at a time.

Preschool (3 -6 years) Adventures: Building Skills One Playtime at a Time

It was Arya's first day at a new playgroup. Her mom, Priya, watched as the other children jumped into games, shared crayons, and chattered away. Arya, however, sat quietly in a corner, her favourite stuffed bunny clutched tightly. Priya's heart ached, but she knew that this was just the start of Arya's journey. She had seen how small, thoughtful activities at home—like playing with blocks or reading stories together—had brought out Arya's giggles and curiosity. Now, it was time to take those skills and help Arya shine in a new environment.

For preschoolers with Autism Spectrum Disorder (ASD), these years are filled with unique opportunities and challenges. From learning to share toys to imagining stories, this stage is about building the foundational skills they'll carry for life. Let's dive into the world of preschoolers and explore how play, patience, and purposeful guidance can unlock their potential.

Why Preschoolers Are Unique

Preschoolers, like Arya, are at an age where their worlds expand beyond home. They encounter new social settings, more complex play, and the chance to grow their budding communication skills. But for children with ASD, navigating these changes can feel overwhelming. This is where thoughtful, age-appropriate activities can make all the difference.

Through structured play, language-building games, and guided social interactions, parents and caregivers can help preschoolers develop the confidence to engage with the world around them, one small step at a time.

Focus Areas for Preschoolers: Unlocking Growth Through Everyday Moments

Preschool is an age of discovery, where little minds and hearts begin to connect with the world around them in more complex ways. For parents of children with Autism Spectrum Disorder (ASD), these years present unique opportunities to nurture language, play, and social skills. Here's how to turn everyday moments into meaningful growth experiences, brought to life through relatable stories.

1. Language Development: From Sounds to Sentences

Story: A Walk with New Words

On a sunny afternoon, Ravi and his mom strolled through the park. Pointing to a bird, she said, "That's a sparrow. Can you say 'bird'?" Ravi smiled and mimicked her, softly saying, "Birrr." As they walked on, they named everything: "tree," "car," and even "dog." Every word Ravi tried became a small victory celebrated with hugs and claps.

How to Practice:

- **Labeling and Naming Objects:** Use everyday opportunities, like pointing out items on a walk or during play, to build vocabulary.

- **Interactive Storytelling:** Pick books with repetitive phrases like *"Brown Bear, Brown Bear, What Do You See?"* Pause and encourage the child to complete the sentence or action.

- **Encouraging Requests:** Keep favorite toys just out of reach so the child uses gestures, pictures, or words to ask for them.

2. Play Skills: Building Creativity and Problem-Solving

Story: The Little Chef's Imagination

"Can you stir the soup?" Priya asked her daughter Arya, handing her a wooden spoon. Arya giggled, pretending to add carrots and salt to the pot. Together, they "cooked" a feast in their pretend kitchen, with Priya gently guiding Arya to take turns adding ingredients. "What's next?" Priya asked, and Arya proudly exclaimed, "Tomato!"

How to Practice:

- **Pretend Play:** Create scenarios like running a pretend kitchen, zoo, or doctor's office to foster imagination.

- **Building with Blocks:** Set goals like "build the tallest tower" or "make a bridge." Celebrate small achievements to build focus and problem-solving skills.

- **Themed Play:** Use toys the child loves, like cars or animals, to create engaging games. For example, pretend the cars are racing or the animals are at a farm.

3. Early Social Interactions: Learning to Share and Connect

Story: Rolling the Ball of Friendship

At a playdate, Arya sat shyly until her mom handed her a ball. "Roll it to Ravi," she encouraged. Arya hesitated but then gently rolled the ball. When Ravi rolled it back, Arya giggled. Soon, the two children were laughing and taking turns, with their moms cheering every interaction.

How to Practice:

- **Turn-Taking Games:** Roll a ball, pass a toy, or play simple board games like *Go Fish* to teach waiting and sharing.

- **Group Storytelling:** Begin with, "Once upon a time, there was a blue car," and let each child add to the story. Gently guide them if they get stuck.

- **Sharing Activities:** During a puzzle, encourage the child to hand a piece to a friend, saying, "Can you help us finish?"

Why These Moments Matter

Preschool years are a time of significant growth, where every interaction is a chance to build skills and confidence. Whether it's naming objects on a walk, cooking up a pretend feast, or learning to share toys, these activities lay the foundation for a lifetime of meaningful connections and learning. Through patience, creativity, and a sprinkle of imagination, parents can help their preschoolers explore, grow, and thrive.

Creating a Supportive Environment for Learning: Turning Everyday Moments into Growth

A supportive environment transforms learning into a joyful experience for preschoolers with Autism Spectrum Disorder (ASD). By blending structure with creativity, parents and caregivers can turn challenges into stepping stones for growth. Let's look at how to create a nurturing space for learning, sprinkled with engaging examples.

1. Use Structured Playtime: Predictability That Sparks Growth

Story: The Magic of a Morning Routine

Each morning, Anya's mom set aside 15 minutes of structured playtime. They began by pretending to run a bakery for five minutes, then tackled a simple puzzle together. To end, Anya had five minutes of free play with her favorite train set. The transitions felt seamless, and Anya flourished in the clear, predictable flow.

How to Practice:

Break playtime into manageable chunks with defined goals. For example, start with five minutes of pretend play, move to a quick puzzle, and finish with unstructured free play. This structure builds focus and fosters a sense of accomplishment.

2. Encourage Interaction with Peers: Building Friendships One Step at a Time

Story: A Game of Shared Laughter

At a small playdate, Liam sat quietly, playing with blocks while another child stacked a tower nearby. Gradually, their parents encouraged a game of "Duck, Duck, Goose." By the second round, Liam was laughing and eagerly waiting for his turn.

How to Practice:

Begin with parallel play, where children engage in individual activities side by side. As they grow more comfortable, introduce simple interactive games like rolling a ball or playing "Duck, Duck, Goose." Gradual progression ensures the child feels safe and supported while learning social skills.

3. Model Appropriate Behavior: Actions Speak Louder Than Words

Story: Sharing the Yellow Crayon

During coloring time, Mia reached for the yellow crayon that her mom was using. Her mom smiled and said, "Here you go, Mia. Would you like to share it with me after you're done?" By watching her mom, Mia learned the value of sharing through action.

How to Practice:

Demonstrate turn-taking, sharing, and polite language during play. Use clear, simple phrases like, "Can I have a turn?" and

"Thank you for sharing!" Children mimic what they see, so modeling kind behavior sets the tone for their interactions.

4. Provide Positive Reinforcement: Celebrate Every Win

Story: The Puzzle Champion

After completing a tricky puzzle with some help, Ethan's mom clapped and said, "Great job finishing the puzzle, Ethan! You worked so hard!" Ethan's face lit up, and he eagerly reached for another puzzle to try.

How to Practice:

Praise specific efforts and behaviors, whether it's waiting their turn, completing a task, or using words to communicate. Rewards can be as simple as a sticker, extra playtime, or a warm hug paired with words like, "I'm so proud of you!"

Why This Matters: Building Foundations for Lifelong Learning

The preschool years are a time of rapid development, where children begin to grasp the fundamentals of communication, play, and social interaction. By incorporating structured playtime, fostering peer connections, modeling behavior, and celebrating progress, parents and caregivers create an environment where growth feels natural and exciting. Every small step forward becomes a building block for future milestones, empowering children to connect with the world and their potential.

From Curiosity to Confidence: Supporting School-Age (6- 12 years) Children with Autism

The Forgotten Lunchbox

Nine-year-old Arjun rushed out the door, excited for a field trip day. Halfway to school, his mom realized he had left his lunchbox on the counter. As she turned the car around, she noticed Arjun growing upset. "I should've remembered!" he said, on the verge of tears. For Arjun, forgetting his lunch wasn't just a mistake—it was a disruption to his carefully built routine, something that felt overwhelming.

For school-age children with Autism Spectrum Disorder (ASD), challenges like these are part of navigating a world filled with new expectations and responsibilities. From managing their first group project to remembering homework, children in this stage encounter a unique blend of academic, social, and personal growth opportunities.

Parents and caregivers often ask: How do we balance supporting their independence while providing the structure they still need? This chapter dives into the critical skills for children aged 6–12, offering practical strategies and relatable stories to help them thrive at home, in school, and in life.

School-age children bring curiosity and a desire for growth, but they also face hurdles that require patience and creativity to overcome. Let's explore ways to turn challenges like Arjun's forgotten lunchbox into teachable moments that build independence, social skills, and confidence.

Focus Areas for School-Age Children: Growth Through Play, Independence, and Connection

1. Building Academic Skills: Learning Beyond the Classroom

The Magic of Snakes and Ladders

Riya struggled to grasp math concepts in a traditional classroom. But one evening, as her family played "Snakes and Ladders," something clicked. Rolling the dice, counting aloud, and moving her token made addition and subtraction fun. When she landed on a ladder and exclaimed, "I went up seven!" her parents realized games could make learning an adventure.

Try This at Home:

- **Board Games for Cognitive Growth:** Introduce games like "Connect Four" or "Scrabble Junior" to teach strategy and vocabulary while keeping the experience playful. Celebrate each move and reinforce the lessons learned during the game.

- **Learning Through Play:** Turn everyday activities into mini-lessons. For example, use a card-matching game to practice sight words or create a scavenger hunt with math riddles.

- **Interactive Reading:** During storytime, ask engaging questions like, "What would you do if you were the hero?" This not only improves comprehension but sparks critical thinking.

2. Encouraging Independence: Confidence in Everyday Actions

The Chore Champion

When Aryan was asked to fold towels, he hesitated. His parents started with one simple step—folding the towel in half. Over time, Aryan took pride in stacking neatly folded towels on the shelf, earning him the title of "Laundry Helper." His newfound confidence extended to brushing his teeth and packing his backpack independently.

Activities to Build Independence:

- **Simple Chores:** Assign tasks like watering plants or setting the table. Break the task into small steps. For example, when setting the table, start with just placing napkins, then add utensils as they gain confidence.

- **Morning Routines with Visual Aids:** Create a checklist with pictures showing steps like brushing teeth, dressing, and packing a school bag. Celebrate small achievements, like completing the checklist on time.

- **Empowering Decisions:** Offer controlled choices, such as "Do you want apple slices or a banana?" Making decisions builds self-esteem and gives the child a sense of control.

3. Fostering Structured Social Interactions: Building Bridges to Friendship

The Lego Bridge Team

During a playdate, Ishaan and his friend worked on a Lego project. Ishaan initially wanted to build alone but, with gentle encouragement, took turns placing blocks. "Your turn," he said shyly, handing over a piece. By the end, they had built not just a bridge but also a connection.

Social Interaction Activities:

- **Collaborative Projects:** Engage in teamwork with activities like creating crafts or assembling puzzles. Start small—perhaps building a tower with blocks—and gently guide sharing and task division.

- **Sports for Social Growth:** Enroll your child in beginner's classes for soccer or swimming. Structured settings teach following instructions, taking turns, and cheering for teammates.

- **Game Nights with Friends:** Simple board games like "Uno" or "Memory" are great for practicing patience, turn-taking, and handling emotions. Celebrate moments of good sportsmanship, whether they win or lose.

Creating a Supportive Environment for School-Age Children

Imagine this: Maya's day used to feel overwhelming—jumbled tasks, confusing expectations, and social situations that seemed like puzzles with missing pieces. But with a few thoughtful strategies, her world began to feel more predictable, manageable, and even exciting. Let's explore ways to create an environment where children like Maya can thrive.

1. Use Visual Supports: Painting a Picture of the Day

Maya loved the morning sun but dreaded the unpredictability of the day. Her parents introduced a colorful visual schedule with pictures: a sun for breakfast, a book for homework, and a swing for playtime. Soon, Maya began checking her chart with excitement, eager to see what came next.

What You Can Do:

- Create a daily schedule with images or icons for activities like meals, homework, and playtime.

- Use visual timers to indicate transitions, like moving from play to chores.

Example:

Place a picture of a toothbrush on the chart for morning routines, followed by a school bus for the next step. Celebrate when your child checks off an activity with a smile!

2. Practice Social Scenarios: Rehearsing Real-Life Interactions

At a birthday party, Aiden froze when another child asked, "Can I have that toy?" His mom decided to turn social challenges into a game. Together, they practiced saying, "Sure, here you go!" during pretend play. The next time Aiden shared, his proud grin lit up the room.

How to Practice:

- Role-play situations like asking for help, sharing toys, or saying "thank you."

- Use puppets or dolls to act out scenarios and encourage your child to take the lead.

Example:

Pretend to bump into your child lightly and say, "Oops, I'm sorry!" Then guide them to respond, "It's okay." Reward their effort with a high-five or sticker.

3. Encourage Problem-Solving: Turning Challenges into Opportunities

When Mia spilled her milk, she panicked. Her dad calmly asked, "What do we do when this happens?" Together, they grabbed a towel, cleaned the spill, and high-fived. The next time Mia spilled, she proudly declared, "I'll fix it!"

How to Practice:

- Guide your child through small challenges, like forgetting homework or losing a toy.

- Use step-by-step instructions to help them identify solutions.

Example:

If your child forgets their lunch, practice saying, "I'll ask my teacher for help," reinforcing that solutions are always within reach.

4. Celebrate Successes: Highlighting Every Achievement

When Sam independently folded his laundry for the first time, his parents didn't just praise him—they made a big deal out of it. "You did that all by yourself!" they said, rewarding him with extra playtime. Sam beamed with pride and couldn't wait to try again.

What to Do:

- Use positive reinforcement, like stickers, hugs, or favorite activities, to acknowledge efforts and successes.

- Celebrate both small and big wins, focusing on their progress.

Example:

If your child greets a friend unprompted, say, "I saw how you said hello! That was fantastic!" Positive feedback reinforces their confidence.

Why This Matters

For school-age children with autism, structure and encouragement are like anchors in a busy world. Visual aids, role-playing, problem-solving, and celebrating achievements give them the tools they need to navigate school and everyday life. These strategies not only help them build academic, social, and practical skills but also foster independence and confidence.

With thoughtful support, children like Maya, Aiden, and Sam can face the day with joy, knowing they are equipped to succeed.

Adolescents (12 years and older) and the Path to Independence: the Unique Challenges

The Lunchroom Transformation

Every school day at noon, Emma faced a moment of dread. The bustling cafeteria was a whirlwind of clanging trays, overlapping chatter, and the unspoken puzzle of "Where should I sit?" The noise made her flinch, and the fear of rejection left her standing frozen, clutching her lunch tray like a shield. Emma, a talented 13-year-old with a love for drawing, longed for quiet and connection, but the chaos around her felt like an insurmountable barrier.

One day, her art teacher, noticing her struggles, made a gentle suggestion: "How about sitting with Lily? She loves sketching, too." Hesitant but hopeful, Emma approached Lily the next day. They bonded over their favorite pencils and the way they both loved drawing animals. What once was an overwhelming ordeal transformed into a peaceful time of shared creativity. By the end of the month, Emma wasn't just surviving lunch—she was thriving, her confidence growing with every sketch and smile exchanged.

For teens with Autism Spectrum Disorder (ASD), stories like Emma's reflect the challenges of navigating adolescence. From the pressures of social settings to the expectations of growing independence, each hurdle is an opportunity for growth. With guidance, patience, and tailored strategies, these moments can become stepping stones toward self-assurance and success. Let's explore how parents and caregivers can support adolescents like Emma through these transformative years.

Focus Areas for Adolescents: Guiding Growth Through Stories

1. Developing Vocational Skills

The Breakfast Triumph

Sam, a 15-year-old with a knack for routine but little confidence in the kitchen, faced his first solo cooking challenge: scrambled eggs. With a visual recipe card in hand—complete with step-by-step pictures—he cautiously cracked his first egg. There were some spills and a bit of shell in the mix, but with patient guidance from his mom, Sam stirred the eggs to fluffy perfection. The grin on his face as he presented his dish spoke volumes about his newfound sense of accomplishment. Cooking didn't just teach Sam a skill; it built his confidence for greater independence.

Chores That Empower

Mia, 13, took pride in her weekly task of organizing the family bookshelf. What started as a simple responsibility evolved into her favorite "job." With stickers as rewards for completing tasks, Mia learned to sort by genre and author, developing a sense of ownership and responsibility. The sense of pride she felt when her parents praised her neat work fueled her motivation to take on more household tasks.

Discovering Hobbies for the Future

Ethan loved to tinker with gadgets. Recognizing this, his parents introduced him to beginner coding programs. What began as curiosity about making lights blink turned into a passion for programming. Now, Ethan dreams of creating his own apps, proving how nurturing interests can open doors to vocational opportunities.

2. Emotional Regulation

Journaling Away Frustration

After a tough day at school, where a group project didn't go as planned, Lily, 14, sat down with her emoji journal. Under the "frustrated" emoji, she wrote, "Group didn't listen to my ideas." Her mom joined her, asking, "What do you think would help next time?" Together, they brainstormed solutions, like practicing how to share ideas calmly. Journaling became Lily's favorite way to process emotions and brainstorm strategies.

The Magic of Calm Breathing

Jake, 16, often felt overwhelmed before exams. His teacher taught him a simple breathing exercise: inhale for four counts, hold for four, and exhale for four. The first time he tried it, Jake wasn't sure it would work. But after a few cycles, he felt the tension in his shoulders ease. Now, Jake uses this technique whenever he feels stress creeping in, whether at school or home.

Role-Playing Confidence

When Emma, 12, was teased about her favorite comic book during lunch, she froze, unsure how to respond. At home, her dad suggested role-playing the situation. He pretended to be the teaser, while Emma practiced assertive yet calm responses like, "I like what I like, and that's okay." The next time it happened, Emma delivered her practiced line with confidence, surprising herself and silencing her peers.

3. Fostering Independence

The Timekeeper's Journey

Alex, 14, often forgot his school assignments, leading to last-minute stress. His mom introduced him to a simple visual planner app. Together, they added tasks like "math homework" and "soccer practice" with reminders. One day, Alex surprised his parents by independently adding "buy gift for friend" to his schedule. With each successful week, Alex gained confidence in managing his time, realizing that a little organization could make life smoother.

The Morning Checklist Champion

Ella, 13, disliked being reminded about brushing her teeth or packing her bag. To make her mornings easier, her dad helped her create a colorful hygiene checklist. Each morning, Ella eagerly checked off steps like "wash face" and "put on socks." When she completed her routine without help for a week, she proudly announced, "I don't need reminders anymore!" Her checklist became her secret weapon for independence.

Money Smarts in Action

When Noah, 15, received his first allowance, he often spent it all on snacks. His parents saw this as an opportunity to teach budgeting. They set up three jars: "Save," "Spend," and "Share." One weekend, Noah saved enough to buy a book he'd wanted for weeks. Seeing his patience pay off, he excitedly declared, "Saving feels even better than spending!"

4. Social Media Safety

Learning the Rules of the Digital World

Lily, 16, was excited to join a social media platform but didn't know how to handle negative comments. Her mom role-played scenarios, pretending to be someone posting an unkind message. Together, they practiced responses like, "I'd rather not argue," and discussed when to block or report a user. When Lily faced a real situation online, she confidently handled it, earning her mom's proud smile.

The Privacy Puzzle

Jacob, 12, loved sharing photos of his favorite Lego creations but wasn't aware of privacy risks. His dad showed him how to set his account to private and explained why personal details should stay offline. After adjusting his settings, Jacob confidently shared his creations, knowing his profile was safe.

Spotting Online Traps

Sophia, 14, received an email promising a "free gaming console" but asking for personal information. Her older sister helped her spot the scam by showing examples of phishing emails. "If it sounds too good to be true, it probably is," they joked. Armed with this knowledge, Sophia proudly identified and avoided future online risks.

Building Bridges to Adulthood: Creating a Supportive Environment for Adolescents

1. Encourage Open Communication

The Homework Heart-to-Heart

Josh, a 14-year-old with a love for science, was struggling with math. His mom noticed his frustration and gently asked, "Can I help?" Reluctantly, Josh opened up about how he felt overwhelmed by fractions. Together, they found a YouTube tutorial that made math feel less daunting. With her patient support, Josh not only solved his homework but also gained confidence to tackle new challenges.

2. Use Visual and Step-by-Step Guides

The Snack Success Story

Ella wanted to make her favorite peanut butter sandwich but often forgot the steps. Her dad created a simple, illustrated chart: "1. Get bread. 2. Spread peanut butter. 3. Add jelly." Following the guide, Ella proudly prepared her snack. "I don't need help anymore!" she declared, her face glowing with pride.

3. Reinforce Effort and Achievements

The Pancake Prodigy

When Ava, 15, cooked pancakes for the first time, they weren't perfect—some were too thin, and one burned. Her parents celebrated her effort instead of the flaws, exclaiming, "You made breakfast for the family! That's amazing!" Encouraged by their praise, Ava kept practicing until her pancakes rivaled any diner's.

4. Involve Them in Decision-Making

The Garden Debate

Liam was torn between learning to cook and trying gardening. His mom asked, "Which one excites you more this week?" Liam chose gardening and helped plant tomatoes in the backyard. When the tomatoes ripened, Liam proudly showed off his contribution to the family's meals. Giving him a choice made the activity more meaningful and boosted his confidence.

Why This Matters

Adolescence is a transformative time, and creating a supportive environment helps set the stage for future success. Open communication fosters trust, visual guides encourage independence, and celebrating efforts builds self-esteem. By involving adolescents in decisions, parents empower them to take ownership of their growth, preparing them for a confident transition into adulthood. These strategies not only nurture skills but also strengthen the bond between parent and child during this pivotal stage.

Chapter 16

Beyond the Plate: Nurturing Healthy Eating Habits in Children with Autism

The Mac and Cheese Phase

Liam's parents joked that he could survive on mac and cheese alone—and for a while, he did. At four years old, Liam, a vibrant and curious child with autism, refused to eat anything else. Carrots? Too crunchy. Apples? Too sticky. His parents tried everything, from singing songs at the table to offering his favorite plate, but Liam's food preferences remained unwavering.

One day, his mom decided to try something new. Together, they made mac and cheese in the kitchen. "What if we add a little broccoli for the dinosaurs?" she asked, pretending the green florets were trees for his toy T-rex. To her surprise, Liam hesitated, then took a bite—his first step toward a more varied diet.

For many parents, mealtime can feel like a battlefield, especially when food sensitivities, picky eating, or dietary challenges come into play. But as Liam's story shows, small, creative changes can make a big difference. Let's explore strategies to navigate food challenges and create a balanced diet tailored to your child's unique needs.

Why Food Matters in Autism

The foods your child eats fuel their growth, behavior, and learning. For children with Autism Spectrum Disorder (ASD), certain food preferences or aversions can impact physical health, sensory processing, and emotional well-being. Understanding these challenges—and how to overcome them—can help turn mealtime into a moment of connection and growth.

Turning Food Challenges into Opportunities: Helping Children with Autism Thrive

1. Selective Eating: The "Only White Foods" Phase

Seven-year-old Alex had a diet as pale as the moon—bread, pasta, cheese, and chicken nuggets were all he would eat. Anything colorful was met with a grimace and a firm "No!" His parents were at their wits' end until they tried something new: food art.

One evening, they arranged carrots, cucumbers, and crackers into a happy face on his plate. Alex laughed but still hesitated. "Try just the nose," his mom encouraged, pointing to a carrot. With a giggle, Alex nibbled at the carrot, slowly expanding his menu.

Tip: Pair preferred foods with small portions of new ones, and make trying new items fun and pressure-free.

2. Sensory Sensitivities: The "Yogurt, Please" Request

Emma couldn't get enough of smooth-textured foods like yogurt or pudding but gagged at anything lumpy. One day, her dad decided to help her explore textures in a fun way. He set up a "texture tasting" game, offering foods like apple sauce and mashed bananas with a small spoonful of her beloved yogurt to start.

Emma cautiously dipped her spoon, and while some textures were rejected, others made the cut. Her favorites? Apple sauce and blended soups.

Tip: Respect your child's preferences while introducing variety gradually. Offer small portions of new textures alongside familiar favorites.

3. Food Jags: "The Week of PB&J"

For three weeks, Ethan wanted nothing but peanut butter and jelly sandwiches for every meal. His parents worried about nutrition but decided to lean into his preference while slowly introducing alternatives.

One day, they swapped the bread for a tortilla, then added banana slices. Ethan enjoyed the twist, and soon his "PB&J phase" became a gateway to trying more fruits.

Tip: Keep offering the preferred food but make small tweaks, like adding a dip or changing the presentation, to gently expand your child's palate.

4. Gastrointestinal (GI) Issues: A "Tummy Troubles" Tale

Sophia often complained of tummy aches after meals, and her appetite dwindled. Her parents tracked her diet and noticed patterns—milk and cheese seemed to trigger discomfort. After consulting a pediatrician, they switched to lactose-free options. Sophia's energy improved, and mealtimes became pleasant again.

Tip: Monitor your child's diet and consult a professional if you notice persistent GI issues. Adjusting fiber intake or eliminating certain foods may help.

5. Allergies and Sensitivities: The Mystery of the Rash

After snacks, Max frequently developed a rash. His parents suspected an allergy but weren't sure what was causing it. With their doctor's guidance, they kept a food diary and discovered the culprit—gluten. By transitioning to a gluten-free diet, Max's rash disappeared, and his behavior improved.

Tip: Pay attention to how your child reacts to different foods. Seek professional advice if you suspect allergies or intolerances.

Why It Matters

Navigating food challenges with creativity and patience can turn mealtime struggles into opportunities for growth. By understanding and addressing these challenges, parents can help their child build a more balanced diet, ensuring their health and happiness thrive.

Busting the Myths: Food Restrictions in Autism

The idea that avoiding certain foods—like gluten, sugar, or caffeine—can "cure" or significantly reduce autism symptoms has gained attention over the years. While some parents swear by such dietary changes, it's essential to separate myths from facts. Let's dig into the truth behind these popular claims.

The Gluten-Free Myth

Gluten, a protein found in wheat, barley, and rye, is often labeled as a culprit in autism. Some believe that removing gluten can improve behavior or communication. However, no scientific study has definitively proven this link for the majority of children with Autism Spectrum Disorder (ASD). Unless your child has a diagnosed gluten intolerance or celiac disease, there's no reason to remove this nutrient-rich food group.

The Sugar Debate

Does sugar cause hyperactivity or worsen autism symptoms? Not necessarily. While consuming too much sugar isn't healthy for any child, there's no evidence that it directly affects autism. It's always a good idea to moderate sugary treats, but depriving your child of birthday cake or cookies without a clear reason might not be necessary.

Caffeine Concerns

Caffeine, commonly found in soda or tea, is said to overstimulate children with autism. While caffeine may affect focus or sleep, the impact varies. Moderation is key, and caffeine isn't inherently harmful.

The Bottom Line

Always consult your pediatrician before removing entire food groups from your child's diet. Depriving your child of certain foods without medical guidance can lead to nutritional deficiencies. Every child is unique—what works for one may not work for another. Balanced nutrition, not myths, is the foundation for their growth and happiness.

Creating a Balanced Diet: Nurturing Growth and Development

For children with Autism Spectrum Disorder (ASD), building a balanced diet is like solving a delightful puzzle—each piece contributes to their growth, energy, and well-being. While it may require a pinch of creativity and a dash of patience, the results are worth every effort.

Key Nutritional Goals: The Building Blocks of Health

1. Protein: The Muscle and Brain Builder

Story: Meet Mia, who loves scrambled eggs and chicken nuggets but refuses beans. Her mom turns mealtime into a game by calling beans "brain boosters," sprinkling them into her favorite soups, and celebrating every bite.

Sources: Chicken, eggs, beans, tofu, or fish.

2. Healthy Fats:

Story: Alex, a budding artist, loves avocado toast. His dad also sneaks in ground seeds into smoothies, calling it "super fuel" for Alex's creativity.

Sources: Avocado, nuts, seeds, and olive oil.

3. Vitamins and Minerals: Nature's Colorful Palette

Tip: Blend vegetables into soups or smoothies for veggie-averse kids. Call the green smoothie a "Superhero Shake," like one mom did for her son Leo, who now looks forward to his spinach-packed drink.

Sources: Fruits, vegetables, and fortified cereals.

4. Fiber: Digestion's Secret Weapon

Story: When Sophie struggled with constipation, her family introduced a "Rainbow Challenge." Each fruit or veggie added to her plate counted as points toward her favorite Friday activity.

Sources: Whole grains, fruits, vegetables, and legumes.

Practical Tips for Parents: Serving Nutrition with a Smile

1. **1. Keep Mealtime Routine:**

    Children with autism thrive on predictability. Regular mealtimes and consistent settings reduce anxiety and help them focus on eating.

2. **2. Use Visual Supports:**

    Example: One family uses picture cards showing the meal progression: "sit at the table," "eat," "clean up." These visuals turn mealtime into a predictable, manageable process.

3. **3. Involve the Child in Food Preparation:**

    Story: Anna's dad let her stir batter and sprinkle toppings on a pizza they made together. Seeing her creation gave her the courage to try new toppings.

4. **4. Start Small with New Foods:**

Tip: Add tiny changes to familiar favorites. One mom stirred a spoonful of cheese into her son's plain pasta, calling it "cheesy clouds." He loved it!

5. **5. Use Positive Reinforcement:**

Story: When Adam tried broccoli for the first time, his parents clapped and added a star to his reward chart, showing how every little step forward matters.

Creating a balanced diet is not just about what's on the plate—it's about making food a joyful, stress-free experience. By blending nutrition with creativity, parents can ensure their children grow strong, healthy, and ready to take on the world.

Chapter 17

Common Myths About Autism: Separating Fact from Fiction

The Whispering Classroom

It was parent-teacher night, and Sarah sat nervously as her son Ethan's teacher began to speak. "He's very quiet," the teacher said. "Do you think his autism means he doesn't want friends or can't connect with others?" Sarah felt her heart drop—not because of the question itself, but because it reflected a widespread misunderstanding. Ethan, like many children with Autism Spectrum Disorder (ASD), was eager to make friends but struggled with initiating conversations. Sarah realized then how powerful myths about autism could be, not just for her son, but for everyone who misunderstood him.

Why Myths Matter

Stories like Ethan's are why addressing myths about autism is so crucial. Misconceptions not only affect how others perceive individuals with ASD but also impact the support, acceptance, and understanding they receive. Let's explore these myths and uncover the truths behind them.

This chapter dives into the most common myths surrounding autism, offering clarity and empowering parents and caregivers with facts to better support their children. Together, we can replace misunderstandings with empathy and knowledge, building a world where every child feels seen, understood, and valued.

Common Myths About Autism: Truth Through Stories

Myth 1: Autism Is Caused by Vaccines

The Fear That Started It All

When Maria took her son, Liam, to the doctor for his 12-month vaccinations, a neighbor's comment left her uneasy. "Aren't you worried about autism?" the neighbor whispered. Maria froze, recalling stories she'd read online. The worry gnawed at her until her pediatrician reassured her: "This myth started with a debunked study from 1998. Autism isn't caused by vaccines—scientific research has confirmed that time and again."

The Reality Behind the Myth

The false claim that vaccines, particularly the MMR (measles, mumps, rubella) vaccine, cause autism originated from a now-discredited study. The study was retracted, and its author lost his medical license, but the myth persists.

What Causes Autism?

Autism stems from differences in brain development, often influenced by:

- **Genetics**: Autism frequently runs in families, suggesting a strong hereditary link.

- **Environmental Factors**: Early-life or prenatal conditions may slightly contribute but don't directly cause autism.

Why Vaccines Matter

Maria remembered her pediatrician's words: "Vaccines save lives by protecting against diseases like measles and polio. Fearing autism shouldn't prevent your child from being safeguarded."

Takeaway for Parents

Vaccines don't cause autism. Protecting your child's health with vaccinations is a decision rooted in science, not myths.

Myth 2: Autism Is the Result of Bad Parenting

Breaking Free from the Past

When Sarah heard her mother-in-law murmur, "Maybe he needs more discipline," she felt a pang of guilt. Her son Ethan had been recently diagnosed with autism, and though she knew better, the old stereotype still stung. She later discovered the origin of this damaging idea: the outdated "refrigerator mother" theory, which blamed cold, unloving parenting for autism.

The Reality Behind the Myth

Science has since shattered this belief. Autism is a neurodevelopmental condition present from birth, linked to differences in brain function. Parenting style has no bearing on whether a child develops autism.

Why It Still Lingers

People often look for easy answers to complex conditions. The refrigerator mother theory lingered for decades, causing unjust blame and heartache for parents.

Supporting Parents Today

Sarah found solace in her parenting community. "We're not the cause," one parent shared. "We're their biggest advocates."

Takeaway for Parents

Autism isn't caused by parenting. Recognize the dedication and love you provide as you guide your child's unique journey.

Myth 3: All People with Autism Have Intellectual Disabilities

Breaking Through First Impressions

When David's teacher saw him struggle to answer questions in class, she initially assumed he wasn't grasping the material. But one day, while discussing space exploration, David lit up. He began rattling off facts about rocket trajectories and planetary distances with a level of detail that stunned everyone. It wasn't that David lacked intelligence; he simply needed the right opportunity to showcase his knowledge.

The Reality Behind the Myth

Autism is a spectrum. While some individuals with autism may have intellectual disabilities, many do not. In fact, some excel in specific areas, demonstrating remarkable talents or above-average intelligence.

What Does the Spectrum Mean?

- Autism impacts individuals differently. Some may face challenges in communication or social interaction while excelling in math, art, or music.

- A small percentage have savant skills, showcasing extraordinary abilities in specific domains.

Examples of Strengths

- **Mathematics**: Solving complex problems with ease.

- **Music**: Playing intricate melodies by ear after hearing them once.

- **Art**: Recreating detailed landscapes or portraits from memory.

Message for Parents

Focus on your child's unique strengths. Whether it's programming, storytelling, or building with Legos, every talent deserves recognition and encouragement. Celebrate their victories, big or small.

Myth 4: Autism Is Rare

From Hidden to Recognized

Years ago, Mia's parents struggled to understand her repetitive behaviors and sensory sensitivities. Doctors dismissed their concerns until Mia was finally diagnosed with autism at age six. They learned they weren't alone—other families in their neighborhood were navigating similar experiences. What felt rare was simply underrecognized.

The Reality Behind the Myth

Autism isn't rare. Estimates show that approximately 1 in 100 children worldwide is diagnosed with autism. This increase isn't due to autism becoming more common but rather improved understanding and broader diagnostic criteria.

Why the Numbers Have Changed

- **Better Awareness**: Educators, parents, and healthcare professionals are now more informed about autism.

- **Expanded Definitions**: Modern criteria capture a wider range of symptoms and severities.

Message for Parents

Autism crosses all demographics and cultures. By embracing awareness, we ensure early intervention and better outcomes for children like Mia, creating a community where their unique perspectives shine.

Myth 5: People with Autism Can't Feel or Express Emotions

The Ice Cream Cone Revelation

Lila's parents often worried that their 7-year-old daughter didn't express affection the way they expected. She rarely said "I love you" or hugged spontaneously. One day, Lila surprised her dad by quietly placing her prized ice cream cone in his hand without a word. It was her way of saying, "I care."

The Reality Behind the Myth

Individuals with autism feel emotions deeply. They may express or process these feelings differently, but their emotional world is rich and complex.

How Emotions Are Expressed

1. **Difficulty Verbalizing Feelings**:

   Michael, a 10-year-old, didn't say, "I'm scared" when he heard thunder. Instead, he curled up under a blanket and hummed softly. This was his way of coping and signaling discomfort.

2. **Delayed Responses**:

   After being teased at school, Sarah seemed unaffected at first. Hours later, she began to cry during her favorite TV show, the delay caused by the time it took her to process the situation.

3. **Overwhelming Emotions**:

When excited about a new toy, 8-year-old Theo jumped and flapped his hands. His joy was just as real but expressed in ways others might not expect.

Message for Parents

- Pay attention to your child's unique emotional language.

- Use tools like emotion charts to help them name and understand their feelings.

- Celebrate their efforts to connect, whether through a smile, a shared toy, or sitting nearby.

Myth 6: Autism Can Be "Cured"

The Miracle Cure Trap

When Ethan's parents heard about a "miracle diet" that promised to cure autism, they were tempted. After all, they wanted the best for their son. But weeks of strict meal plans led only to frustration and meltdowns. Ethan wasn't being "cured"; he was just being misunderstood.

The Reality Behind the Myth

Autism isn't a disease that needs curing. It's a neurodevelopmental condition that shapes how a person experiences and interacts with the world. With the right support, individuals with autism can thrive and build meaningful lives.

Why the Myth Persists

Unproven therapies and "miracle cures" exploit parents' hopes, offering promises that lack scientific evidence. True progress comes through evidence-based approaches, like speech therapy, occupational therapy, and behavioral interventions.

Focus on Growth, Not Change

1. **Acceptance Builds Confidence**:

   Jamie's parents embraced her love of animals, enrolling her in a pet care class. Instead of trying to change her, they focused on her strengths, helping her build self-esteem.

2. **Skills Over Cures**:

   Through social skills training, Ryan, who struggled with conversations, learned to greet classmates and make friends. His autism didn't disappear, but his ability to navigate the world improved dramatically.

Message for Parents

- Be wary of "quick fixes" or therapies with bold but unsupported claims.

- Embrace interventions that focus on helping your child grow and succeed.

- Celebrate their individuality. Autism brings unique strengths and perspectives to the world, and your child is no exception.

Myth 7: People with Autism Don't Want Relationships or Friendships

The Playground Partner

Eight-year-old Sam loved dinosaurs. At recess, while other kids played tag, he sat in a corner arranging his dinosaur toys. One day, another child approached and asked, "Can I play too?" Sam didn't respond with words but slid a toy toward the child, inviting them into his world without saying a word. Over time, Sam and his new friend created entire dinosaur adventures together.

The Reality

Children with autism often crave friendships and relationships but may express this desire in nontraditional ways. While verbal communication or eye contact might not come easily, actions like sharing a favorite toy or sitting close to someone are meaningful gestures of connection.

What Parents Should Know

- Children with autism might need support to navigate social norms, such as turn-taking or initiating conversations.

- Social skills training can empower them to build and maintain friendships.

Message for Parents

- Encourage structured social activities, like playdates with clear goals or group projects.

- Celebrate every step, from a smile to a simple "hello." Relationships might take longer to form but are deeply valued.

Myth 8: Autism Is Always Visible

The Class Clown with a Hidden Struggle

Lila was the class clown. She loved making her classmates laugh with funny voices and jokes. But at home, her parents noticed how exhausted she was after school. Lila struggled to decode sarcasm, felt overwhelmed in noisy environments, and often needed hours alone to recharge.

The Reality

Autism isn't always visible. While some traits, like repetitive movements or nonverbal communication, are more apparent, others, like social anxiety or sensory challenges, might be hidden. Individuals with autism often mask their struggles in public, leading others to assume they don't face difficulties.

What Parents Should Know

- Children who "blend in" socially may still find interactions exhausting or confusing.

- Even highly verbal or academically gifted children can have significant challenges that aren't immediately obvious.

Message for Parents

- Advocate for your child's needs, even if they appear neurotypical to others.

- Help teachers and peers understand that autism is a spectrum, with strengths and challenges that aren't always visible.

- Encourage environments where your child feels safe being themselves, without the pressure to hide their difficulties.

Empowering Your Journey

By understanding these myths and the truths behind them, parents and caregivers can better support their children with autism. Celebrate your child's unique ways of connecting, growing, and thriving. Whether they're building quiet friendships or navigating unseen struggles, your encouragement and advocacy make all the difference.

How Myths Impact Families

A Day at the Park

Maya had taken her son, Liam, to the park for some playtime. As Liam spun happily on the merry-go-round, another parent whispered, "Why doesn't he talk to the other kids? Is he shy or something?" Maya tried to explain that Liam was on the autism spectrum and expressed himself differently, but the other parent just shrugged and muttered, "He doesn't look autistic to me." Maya left the park feeling judged and isolated, wishing people understood her son's uniqueness instead of relying on harmful myths.

The Ripple Effect of Myths

Myths about autism don't just misinform—they create barriers. These misconceptions can lead to:

- **Dismissed Needs:** People may overlook a child's struggles because their autism isn't "obvious."

- **Blame on Parents:** Harmful beliefs about bad parenting can leave families feeling unfairly judged.

- **Exclusion:** Misunderstandings may lead to social isolation, as people avoid engaging with families out of fear or ignorance.

For parents, this can result in loneliness, frustration, and the exhausting need to constantly explain their child's behavior.

What Parents Can Do

Turning Misunderstanding into Teaching Moments

When Emma's classmate didn't invite her to a birthday party because her mom thought Emma's "meltdowns might ruin the fun," Emma's parents saw an opportunity. They gently explained that Emma's sensory challenges sometimes led to meltdowns, but she thrived in smaller groups. They invited the family over for a playdate, helping them see Emma's sweet, funny personality firsthand.

Steps to Break the Cycle

1. **Educate Others:**

   - Share reliable resources and explain that autism is a spectrum.

   - Help people understand that strengths and challenges vary for each individual.

2. **Advocate for Your Child:**

   - Partner with schools and communities to ensure your child's needs are met.

   - Stand up to stereotypes by providing real-life examples of your child's abilities and challenges.

3. **Encourage Open Conversations:**

   - Create a judgment-free zone where friends and family can ask respectful questions.

   - Share your child's milestones and achievements to break down misconceptions.

Example: If someone says, "But your child doesn't seem autistic," use it as a teaching moment. Explain how autism affects each person differently, from sensory sensitivities to social interactions, and highlight your child's unique strengths.

Breaking the Cycle of Myths

A Community of Understanding

When Liam started school, Maya made a point to meet with his teacher and classmates' parents to explain autism in simple, relatable terms. She shared stories of Liam's progress, from learning to tie his shoes to saying "hello" to his neighbors. Slowly, the whispers at the park turned into smiles and waves.

Why It Matters

Myths about autism perpetuate stigma and misunderstandings, limiting opportunities for individuals with autism to thrive.

When parents and caregivers step forward to educate others, they create a ripple effect of acceptance and inclusion.

Fostering Understanding

- Autism is not something to fear or pity—it's a unique way of experiencing the world.

- Every individual with autism has abilities and potential that enrich their families and communities.

Message for Parents:

You are your child's greatest advocate and the key to breaking down misconceptions. By sharing their journey, celebrating their progress, and standing up for their potential, you're paving the way for a world that values and supports individuals with autism. Acceptance begins with awareness—and you are leading the charge.

Chapter 18

Pathways to Progress: Treatment Options for Autism

A Mother's Leap of Faith

When Priya's son Aarav was diagnosed with Autism Spectrum Disorder (ASD) at age three, she felt overwhelmed. Aarav was bright and curious but struggled to communicate his needs, often leading to meltdowns that left both mother and son in tears. A friend recommended starting speech therapy, but Priya hesitated—would it work for Aarav? Would he understand? Desperate to help her son, she decided to try.

Within months, Aarav was using simple words like "juice" and "play" to express himself. The meltdowns became less frequent, replaced with moments of connection and joy. Priya realized that the right support wasn't just about teaching Aarav skills; it was about unlocking his world.

This is the transformative power of tailored treatments for autism. They don't erase the challenges but equip children and families with tools to navigate them together. Let's explore how individualized therapies can make a profound difference.

Understanding Autism Treatment

Why Early Intervention Matters

Treatment for autism isn't about finding a cure—it's about providing support to help individuals thrive. Research shows that early intervention can significantly improve communication, social, and cognitive abilities.

Example:

When Aarav started therapy at three, he initially resisted the structured activities. But his therapist used his love of cars to build a communication bridge. By age four, Aarav was pointing to toy cars and saying their colors—a milestone that filled his family with hope.

Message for Parents:

The earlier you begin tailored interventions, the greater the potential for positive outcomes. It's not just about skill-building; it's about fostering confidence and connection.

Importance of Individualized Treatment

Every Child's Journey is Unique

Autism manifests differently in each child. For this reason, treatment plans must be personalized to suit their strengths, challenges, and interests.

Example:

Meera, a bubbly five-year-old, excelled in visual tasks but struggled with verbal communication. Her parents worked with a therapist to integrate picture-based communication tools into her daily routine. Over time, Meera began using picture cards to express her needs, reducing her frustration and fostering her independence.

Message for Parents:

There is no "one-size-fits-all" solution. Partner with professionals to craft a treatment plan as unique as your child, focusing on their abilities and developmental goals.

Priya's leap of faith with Aarav wasn't just about trying a therapy; it was about believing in his potential. The right treatment can empower children with autism to overcome obstacles and build the skills they need to shine in their unique way.

Understanding Behavioral and Developmental Therapies

The Magic of Early Intervention

A Story About the Right Start

Two-year-old Aanya didn't respond when her name was called and avoided eye contact. Her parents, unsure of how to support her, enrolled her in an early intervention program.

Aanya's weekly therapy sessions included ABA to teach her how to follow simple instructions, speech therapy to help her vocalize needs, and occupational therapy to manage sensory sensitivities. Her therapists worked together, focusing on small, achievable goals like pointing to a toy she wanted or clapping during a song.

After a few months, Aanya began reaching for her parents to play and babbling during familiar songs. Her parents felt a new sense of hope, seeing the progress unfold before their eyes.

What Early Intervention Offers:

Early intervention leverages the critical developmental years when the brain is most adaptable. By combining therapies, it targets skills like communication, motor abilities, and social interaction.

Message for Parents:

Starting early doesn't just build skills—it opens doors to better communication, less frustration, and stronger connections with your child. Think of it as giving them a toolbox for life.

The Power of Rewards: Applied Behavior Analysis (ABA)

A Story About Positive Reinforcement

When six-year-old Aryan started ABA therapy, he rarely made eye contact or used words to ask for things. His therapist noticed that Aryan loved toy trains. Using positive reinforcement, the therapist introduced a simple task: saying "train" to get his favorite toy.

At first, Aryan hesitated, pointing to the train instead of saying the word. With gentle encouragement and clear prompts, Aryan finally said "train." Immediately, the therapist handed him the toy and cheered, "Great job saying 'train'!" Over time, Aryan began using other words like "ball" and "juice," excited by the rewards and recognition he received.

What ABA Does:

ABA breaks tasks into small, manageable steps (task analysis) and uses positive reinforcement to teach new skills.

Example Technique:

Teaching handwashing involves teaching one step at a time:

1. Turning on the tap.

2. Rubbing soap on hands.

3. Rinsing under water.

4. Drying hands with a towel.

Message for Parents:

ABA isn't about rigid drills; it's tailored to your child's needs. Whether it's learning to communicate, dress independently, or play with friends, ABA builds skills in a fun, rewarding way.

DIR/Floortime: Building Connections Through Play

A Story About Meeting Your Child Where They Are

When three-year-old Aarav played with his toy cars, he always lined them up neatly and avoided anyone who tried to join him. His parents felt unsure about how to connect with him until they began DIR/Floortime therapy.

One day, Aarav's therapist sat beside him, picked up a car, and quietly started lining it up like Aarav did. Aarav glanced at the therapist but didn't resist. After a few minutes, the therapist gently introduced a challenge: "Let's race the cars!" Aarav hesitated but eventually rolled a car forward. The therapist praised him with excitement, and soon Aarav was laughing as they raced cars together.

What DIR/Floortime Does:

DIR/Floortime focuses on joining the child at their developmental level. By turning activities they already enjoy into opportunities for interaction, it fosters emotional bonds and builds essential skills.

Message for Parents:

Play isn't just play—it's a chance to connect, teach problem-solving, and encourage communication in a way that feels natural and joyful.

Social Skills Training: Preparing for Real-World Interactions

A Story About Building Bridges to Friendship

Seven-year-old Mia loved playing on the swings but avoided talking to other kids at the park. During her social skills training, her therapist introduced role-playing games.

In one session, the therapist practiced saying "hello" with Mia by shaking hands and making eye contact. Later, during a group activity, Mia joined other children to build a Lego tower. The therapist guided her, suggesting phrases like, "Can I have the red block?" With practice, Mia gained confidence in talking to her peers.

One afternoon at the park, Mia surprised her mom by asking another child, "Can I play too?" and joining a game of tag.

What Social Skills Training Does:

Social skills training helps children learn and practice the rules of social interaction in a safe, supportive environment. Role-playing and group activities teach children how to communicate, take turns, and understand social cues.

Message for Parents:

Every child wants to connect—they just need the tools to do it. Social skills training builds confidence and opens the door to friendships and meaningful relationships.

Explaining Speech Therapy

Speech Therapy: Unlocking Communication

A Story About Finding a Voice

Six-year-old Rahul struggled to express his needs, often becoming frustrated when he couldn't find the words. During his first speech therapy session, his therapist introduced the Picture Exchange Communication System (PECS). They began with simple cards showing images of everyday items like water and snacks.

One day, Rahul pointed to the card for "cookie" and handed it to the therapist. With a big smile, the therapist praised him, saying, "Great job asking for a cookie!" Rahul's face lit up as he realized he could make his needs known.

As weeks passed, Rahul started forming short phrases, turning "cookie" into "I want a cookie." Each small milestone brought visible joy to Rahul and his parents, who practiced these skills with him at home.

Message for Parents:

Speech therapy opens doors to communication, helping children express themselves in ways that reduce frustration and strengthen bonds with others. Your involvement in practicing these skills is essential to their success.

Educational Interventions: Setting the Stage for Success

A Story About Personalized Learning

Meera, an eight-year-old with autism, loved drawing but found reading challenging. Her school created an Individualized Education Plan (IEP) to support her needs. The plan included visual aids for reading lessons and regular breaks to help her stay focused.

During one session, her teacher used picture books about animals—Meera's favorite topic. With visual prompts and encouragement, Meera began identifying words like "lion" and "zebra." Her teacher also incorporated art projects to keep Meera engaged, such as creating animal-themed storyboards.

Meera's parents worked closely with the school to review her progress every month. They shared feedback and celebrated her successes, like reading her first sentence aloud.

What an IEP Does:

An IEP is a personalized educational roadmap. It sets specific goals and provides accommodations tailored to a child's strengths and challenges.

Message for Parents:

Collaborating with educators ensures your child receives the support they need to thrive. Don't hesitate to advocate for their needs or suggest strategies that align with their interests.

By integrating speech therapy and educational interventions, families can empower their children to overcome challenges and reach their full potential. These tailored approaches build confidence, unlock communication, and create a foundation for lifelong learning.

Role of Inclusive and Specialized Classrooms

Education settings can vary widely for children with autism, and the choice depends on their needs and abilities.

Inclusive Classrooms:

- In an inclusive setting, children with autism learn alongside neurotypical peers. This environment fosters social interaction and helps children practice communication and adaptive skills.

- **Example**: A child with mild social challenges might participate in a mainstream classroom with the support of a teaching assistant or modified lessons.

Specialized Classrooms:

- These classrooms provide a smaller, more structured environment tailored to children with autism or other developmental delays.

- **Example**: A specialized class might use visual schedules, sensory breaks, and individualized instruction to meet the needs of each child.

Message for Parents: Discuss your child's learning style and needs with educators to determine the best placement. Some children thrive in inclusive settings, while others benefit from the focused attention of a specialized classroom.

Occupational Therapy for Autism: Understanding Through Stories

The Sensory Diet: A Personalized Path to Calm

The Story of Aryan

Aryan, a seven-year-old with autism, struggled to focus in school. Bright lights and the chatter of classmates often overwhelmed him, leading to meltdowns. His occupational therapist introduced a "sensory diet," a series of calming activities tailored to his needs.

Before school, Aryan spent five minutes on a mini-trampoline, which helped him release pent-up energy. During class, he wore a weighted vest that made him feel grounded and used a stress ball when the noise became too much. Over time, these strategies helped Aryan stay calm and engaged, making his school days more manageable.

Message for Parents:

A sensory diet provides your child with tools to manage their environment. Ask your occupational therapist about activities and tools you can incorporate into daily routines to create a sense of balance.

Adaptive Tools: Small Changes, Big Impact

The Story of Meera

Meera found noisy environments like grocery stores unbearable. During OT sessions, she was introduced to noise-canceling headphones. Her therapist explained how these could block overwhelming sounds, giving Meera a sense of control. Armed with her headphones, Meera began accompanying her mother on short shopping trips. Soon, she was even helping pick out her favorite snacks.

Message for Parents:

Adaptive tools like fidget toys or headphones empower children to handle sensory challenges. Experiment with options to find what works best for your child.

Building Independence Through Self-Care Skills

The Story of Kabir

Kabir, a five-year-old, had difficulty dressing himself. His occupational therapist used a button board to practice fastening buttons in a fun and stress-free way. They gradually moved to real shirts, celebrating small wins like buttoning one sleeve. Within weeks, Kabir could proudly dress himself for school.

Message for Parents:

Reinforce self-care skills at home by turning daily tasks into learning opportunities. Use tools like step-by-step visual charts or practice sessions to build confidence.

Fine Motor Skills and Handwriting: Making Everyday Tasks Easier

The Story of Ananya

Ananya struggled to hold a pencil and write her name. Her occupational therapist introduced playdough exercises to strengthen her hand muscles. They also used a pencil grip to help her practice writing. Soon, Ananya could write her name clearly, beaming with pride each time she showed her parents.

Message for Parents:

Fine motor exercises like squeezing playdough or threading beads can improve your child's dexterity. Incorporate these activities into playtime to make learning enjoyable.

Occupational therapy is not just about treatment sessions; it's about equipping children with the tools and confidence to navigate their world. By reinforcing OT strategies at home, you can help your child become more independent, adaptable, and ready to face daily challenges. Celebrate every small step—each one is a stride toward greater independence!

Augmentative and Alternative Communication (AAC): Empowering Voices Through Stories

The Power of Pictures

The Story of Riya

Riya, a four-year-old with autism, often grew frustrated when she couldn't express her needs. This led to meltdowns during mealtime, as her parents struggled to understand what she wanted. During therapy, Riya was introduced to the Picture Exchange Communication System (PECS).

One day, she held up a picture of a sandwich from her PECS folder and handed it to her dad. The moment he responded by preparing her favorite peanut butter sandwich, her face lit up with joy. The family began using PECS for daily routines, and Riya's frustration eased as her ability to communicate blossomed.

Message for Parents:

Start small by using pictures of your child's favorite items. Gradually expand to include daily activities and feelings to encourage broader communication.

Speaking Through Technology

The Story of Aarav

Aarav, an eight-year-old who was non-verbal, felt isolated in group settings. His therapist introduced him to a tablet with a speech-generating app. Aarav quickly learned to type phrases like "I want to play" or "I need help." One day, during a family gathering, he proudly used the app to say, "Thank you for the cake," melting everyone's hearts.

Message for Parents:

Explore communication apps tailored to your child's needs. Practice during family time to build confidence and strengthen connections.

Simple Tools, Big Results

The Story of Samaira

Samaira struggled to express her daily choices. Her therapist provided a low-tech communication board with pictures of activities like eating, playing, and resting. During playtime, Samaira pointed to the "blocks" image, showing her preference for building towers. Over time, her ability to make choices improved dramatically.

Message for Parents:

Low-tech options like boards are cost-effective and easy to use. Pair them with verbal cues to support language development.

Key Takeaway for Parents

AAC tools are bridges to understanding and connection. Start with tools your child feels comfortable with and celebrate each milestone, knowing you're giving them the gift of expression and independence.

Chapter 19

When to Consider Medication: Stories of Hope and Help

Anxiety: Breaking Free from Fear

The Story of Maya

Maya, a bright 7-year-old with autism, began dreading her school mornings. She would cling to her mother, crying, overwhelmed by the thought of noisy hallways and crowded classrooms. Despite her parents and teachers trying sensory-friendly strategies and gradual exposure, Maya's anxiety remained unmanageable.

Her pediatrician recommended medication to complement her ongoing therapy. Within weeks, Maya's parents noticed a change—she was calmer, able to enter her classroom without tears, and even started participating in group activities.

Message for Parents:

Medication isn't about "fixing" your child; it's about providing a tool to ease overwhelming emotions so they can thrive.

ADHD: Finding Focus in a Busy World

The Story of Rohan

Rohan loved puzzles, but in school, he couldn't focus long enough to finish even simple tasks. His teacher described him as "constantly in motion," fidgeting, tapping, and jumping from one activity to another. His parents tried structured routines and positive reinforcement, but Rohan's struggles persisted.

After a thorough evaluation, Rohan's doctor prescribed ADHD medication. With this support, Rohan could focus better in class and even discovered a love for building complex Lego structures at home.

Message for Parents:

Medication for ADHD isn't a shortcut; it's a way to help your child harness their strengths and explore their potential.

Epilepsy: Navigating Seizures with Confidence

The Story of Aisha

Aisha had always been an active child, but her parents began noticing moments when she would "zone out," staring blankly for several seconds. One day, she experienced a convulsion during playtime, leading to a diagnosis of epilepsy.

Medication helped control Aisha's seizures, giving her and her family peace of mind. With her seizures managed, Aisha returned to her favorite activities, including riding her bike and baking cookies with her mom.

Message for Parents:

Seizure management through medication can provide stability, ensuring your child stays safe while enjoying life's moments.

Severe Behavioral Challenges: Reclaiming Calm

The Story of Liam

Liam's meltdowns were intense and frequent, often resulting in him hitting his head against the wall or lashing out at his parents. Despite therapy and a carefully crafted behavioral plan, Liam's frustration seemed beyond his control, leaving his family feeling helpless.

A child psychiatrist prescribed medication to help regulate Liam's mood. Gradually, the intensity of his meltdowns reduced, allowing him to engage more fully in his therapy sessions and bond with his parents during playtime.

Message for Parents:

Medication can create a window of calm, enabling your child to benefit more from other interventions and enjoy their relationships.

Common Medications: Stories of Support and Progress

Medications can play a crucial role in managing the symptoms or co-occurring conditions associated with autism. The goal is not to "fix" autism but to address specific challenges that may hinder a child's daily life. Here's how medications can help, illustrated with relatable stories for parents.

1. Medications for Anxiety and Depression: Finding Calm

Lila's Constant Worries

Lila, a thoughtful 10-year-old, couldn't stop asking her mom, "What if I mess up my project?"—not once, but 20 times in an hour. Her repetitive questioning was driven by intense anxiety, leaving her unable to focus or enjoy her favorite activities.

Her doctor prescribed an SSRI, such as Fluoxetine (Prozac). Over time, Lila became more relaxed and confident. She still cared about her project but could now ask her question once and move forward with excitement.

How They Help: SSRIs like Fluoxetine or Sertraline (Zoloft) regulate mood, reducing obsessive behaviors and repetitive thoughts.

2. Medications for ADHD Symptoms: Unlocking Focus

Eli's Endless Energy

Eli loved dinosaurs but couldn't sit still long enough to finish a dinosaur puzzle in class. He'd dart from activity to activity, leaving his teachers and parents concerned about his learning.

With a stimulant like Methylphenidate, Eli learned to channel his energy. Soon, he was completing his puzzles and proudly showing them to his classmates.

Non-Stimulant Options: For children like Mia, who experienced side effects with stimulants, Atomoxetine provided a gentler alternative while improving focus.

3. Medications for Severe Behavioral Challenges: Easing Aggression

Noah's Tough Days

Noah's meltdowns often involved screaming and hitting when he felt overwhelmed. His parents tried everything from calming techniques to therapy, but his aggression put him and others at risk.

His doctor recommended Risperidone, an antipsychotic. Within weeks, Noah's meltdowns became less frequent and less intense, allowing him to engage in therapy and learn new coping strategies.

How They Help: Antipsychotics like Risperidone or Aripiprazole manage severe irritability, aggression, and self-injury.

4. Medications for Seizure Management: Keeping Safe

Ava's Quiet Episodes

Ava's parents were worried about her frequent staring spells during playtime, later diagnosed as absence seizures. These brief moments interrupted her learning and interactions.

With Valproate, Ava's seizures were reduced significantly. She now stays present in activities, building her first block towers with glee.

How They Help: Anti-seizure medications control and reduce seizure frequency, improving attention and safety.

5. Sleep Aids: Restoring Rest

Leo's Long Bedtimes

Bedtime was a struggle for Leo, who would toss and turn for hours. His sleepless nights left him cranky and unfocused during the day.

A pediatrician recommended melatonin, a natural supplement. With this support, Leo began falling asleep faster and waking up refreshed, ready to tackle his day.

How They Help: Sleep aids like melatonin can help children settle into a consistent sleep routine.

The Importance of Monitoring: A Parent's Guide to Medication for Autism

When Lily's parents noticed her behavior improving with medication, they felt a wave of relief. But after a few weeks, they observed that she seemed unusually sleepy during the day. Concerned, they scheduled a follow-up with her doctor. This small adjustment—lowering her dosage—brought balance to Lily's routine and restored her energy. Stories like Lily's highlight why monitoring medication is essential for children with autism.

Why Monitoring Matters

Medication can make a significant difference for children with Autism Spectrum Disorder (ASD), but it's not a "set it and forget it" solution. Every child reacts differently to medications, and careful observation ensures that benefits outweigh any side effects.

Regular Medical Follow-Ups: Fine-Tuning Success

Children's needs evolve, and medications may require adjustments over time.

- **Example:** Jake's irritability improved with risperidone, but his parents noticed rapid weight gain. At their follow-up, the doctor adjusted the dosage and suggested dietary changes to help maintain a healthy weight.

Tip: Schedule consistent check-ins with your child's prescribing doctor to review progress and address concerns.

Watching for Side Effects: The Parent's Role

Side effects can be subtle or immediate, and tracking changes is key to addressing them promptly.

- **Common side effects:** Drowsiness, irritability, appetite changes, or digestive issues.

- **Tip:** Keep a journal to log your child's behaviors, symptoms, and any changes after starting or adjusting medication.

Example: Mia's ADHD medication improved her focus but disrupted her sleep. A bedtime routine tweak and adjusted timing of doses resolved the issue.

Balancing Risks and Benefits: Finding the Sweet Spot

Every medication decision involves weighing the positives against potential challenges.

- **Example:** For Ethan, ADHD medication reduced hyperactivity but led to mild stomach upset. His doctor recommended taking the medication with food, balancing its benefits with manageable side effects.

Conclusion: A Path to Progress

Medications can be a powerful part of a child's treatment plan when combined with careful monitoring.

- **Message for Parents:** Stay involved. Regular communication with healthcare providers ensures that your child's medication continues to support their growth and well-being.

With vigilance and collaboration, medication can be an effective tool to enhance a child's quality of life, empowering them to thrive in their unique journey. Always consult trusted healthcare professionals to make informed decisions tailored to your child's needs.

Chapter 20

Beyond Conventional: Exploring Alternative Approaches for Autism

The Healing Power of Connection

Six-year-old Sofia had always been a mystery to her parents. She preferred the quiet company of her toys to the chatter of family gatherings, and her smiles were fleeting, almost as if they were afraid to linger. When her therapist suggested alternative therapies, her parents hesitated, unsure if these unfamiliar methods could really help.

But everything changed one rainy afternoon. In a cozy music therapy room filled with drums, tambourines, and maracas, Sofia sat quietly, observing. The therapist picked up a tambourine and tapped it softly to the rhythm of a familiar tune. At first, Sofia simply watched, her curiosity piqued. Then, tentatively, she reached out and held the tambourine, her small fingers brushing against the smooth metal discs.

"Would you like to try?" the therapist gently asked. Sofia hesitated but then, almost as if drawn by the beat, gave the tambourine a soft shake. The sound filled the room, and something magical happened—Sofia smiled. Not a fleeting smile, but a beaming, joyful expression that lit up her face. Encouraged, she began tapping the tambourine in rhythm, her smile growing with each beat. Her parents watched with tears in their eyes, witnessing a connection they had long hoped for.

That tambourine was more than an instrument; it was a bridge into Sofia's world. Stories like hers illustrate how alternative therapies can open doors to communication, expression, and joy for children with Autism Spectrum Disorder (ASD), creating moments of connection that ripple far beyond the therapy room.

Sensory Integration Therapy: Navigating the Sensory World

Imagine Noah, a seven-year-old with autism, walking into a bustling grocery store. The bright fluorescent lights feel like strobe lights to him, the hum of carts clashing sounds deafening, and the textures of cold metal shelves and rough paper bags are overwhelming. Overstimulated, Noah curls into a ball, shielding himself from the chaos. His parents feel helpless, wondering how to make the world a little easier for him to navigate.

This is where **Sensory Integration Therapy (SIT)** steps in—a lifeline for children like Noah who struggle with sensory sensitivities. Designed to help kids process sensory information more effectively, SIT is tailored to their unique needs, teaching them to tolerate and adapt to their environment.

How It Works: Therapy Through Play

A trained occupational therapist transforms therapy into a fun and engaging experience. Tools like swings, balance boards, and textured materials are carefully chosen to address a child's specific sensory challenges. Over time, these activities can improve focus, emotional regulation, and motor coordination.

For Hyper-Sensitivity: Easing Overwhelm

Sofia, who finds bright lights and loud sounds unbearable, begins therapy in a softly lit room with calming textures. The therapist hands her a soft, textured ball to squeeze, introducing her to new sensations in a controlled, soothing way. Soon, she's able to handle brighter environments without feeling overwhelmed.

For Hypo-Sensitivity: Seeking Stimulation

Then there's Lucas, an energetic eight-year-old who craves sensory input, spinning endlessly on his own. In therapy, he jumps on a trampoline and swings in a hammock, activities that provide the stimulation he needs while helping him regulate his body's balance system. Over time, these sessions reduce his need for constant movement.

Tips for Parents

1. Create a Sensory-Friendly Space

At home, Noah's parents set up a cozy sensory corner with weighted blankets, noise-canceling headphones, and a box of sensory-friendly toys. It becomes his go-to spot when the world feels too much.

2. Incorporate into Daily Life

Lucas's parents add sensory activities to his routine, like squeezing playdough while waiting for dinner or jumping on a trampoline before school to release excess energy.

Why It Matters

Studies have found that SIT reduces sensory-related behaviors and improves functional skills in children with autism. For Noah, it's more than therapy—it's a bridge to a calmer, more manageable world. His parents watch as he begins to handle trips to the grocery store with newfound confidence, exploring the aisles rather than shrinking from them.

Sensory Integration Therapy doesn't just teach children to cope; it empowers them to thrive in their sensory-rich environments, opening doors to greater independence and joy.

Music and Art Therapy: Unlocking Expression Through Creativity

The Quiet Drummer

Ethan, a non-verbal six-year-old with autism, often retreated into his own world, avoiding eye contact and struggling to connect with others. During his first music therapy session, his therapist handed him a drum. Initially hesitant, Ethan tapped the drum timidly. Encouraged by the therapist's rhythm, he began to tap more confidently, matching the beats. Soon, Ethan was smiling as he played, his eyes lighting up with a sense of achievement. This moment was the first step in fostering connection and communication through music.

Music and art therapy offer powerful tools to help children like Ethan express themselves, build confidence, and develop essential skills. These therapies tap into a child's natural curiosity and creativity, fostering growth in a way that feels playful and non-threatening.

Music Therapy: Building Connections Through Sound

How It Works

Music therapists use melodies, rhythms, and instruments to engage children. Activities like singing, playing simple instruments, or moving to music encourage interaction and help teach skills like turn-taking or following directions.

Evidence

A 2022 study in *Frontiers in Psychology* found that music therapy significantly improved communication, social skills, and emotional regulation in children with autism.

Example

During a session, Ethan's therapist used a drum to encourage interaction. With each tap, the therapist mirrored his rhythm, creating a musical "conversation." Over time, Ethan began to initiate his own beats, using the drum as a way to communicate.

Art Therapy: Expressing the Inexpressible

How It Works

Art therapy provides children with a visual and tactile medium to express emotions and ideas. Through activities like painting, drawing, or sculpting, children can communicate feelings they might struggle to verbalize.

Evidence

Researches highlight art therapy's ability to reduce anxiety and improve self-expression in children with autism.

Example

Sophia, an eight-year-old who struggled to articulate her emotions, used crayons to draw pictures of her favorite activities. One day, she drew her family holding hands under a rainbow, giving her parents a glimpse into her feelings of love and connection.

Tips for Parents

1. **Encourage Creativity at Home**

   Provide simple materials like crayons, paints, or drums to let your child explore music and art in a relaxed environment.

   Example: During downtime, set up a small art station with paper and washable markers for your child to enjoy freely.

2. **Focus on Process, Not Perfection**

   Celebrate your child's effort and engagement rather than critiquing the final result.

Example: If your child paints a messy rainbow, praise their use of colors and enthusiasm, rather than focusing on neatness.

Why It Matters

Music and art therapy help children with autism break down communication barriers, express emotions, and foster connections. For Ethan, a drumbeat became a bridge to the world around him, showing that with the right tools, every child can find their unique voice.

Animal-Assisted Therapy: A Unique Bond That Heals

Sam's New Friend

Sam, a nine-year-old with autism, often felt anxious in social situations. One day, his parents introduced him to Max, a gentle therapy dog. At first, Sam was hesitant, but Max patiently sat by his side. Over time, Sam began to pet Max, smile, and even whisper commands like "sit." This simple interaction sparked a change—Sam started looking forward to his sessions with Max, gaining confidence and showing more interest in engaging with others.

Animal-assisted therapy builds connections like the one between Sam and Max, providing emotional comfort and teaching valuable social and emotional skills.

How Animal-Assisted Therapy Works

Animals create a non-judgmental and calming environment for some children with autism. Interacting with animals helps reduce anxiety, improve emotional regulation, and encourage communication skills. Activities such as walking a dog, grooming a horse, or feeding a guinea pig can become therapeutic experiences.

Evidence

Researches have found that children with autism who participated in animal-assisted therapy displayed reduced anxiety and increased social engagement. Interaction with animals also lowers cortisol levels, reducing stress.

Examples of Animal-Assisted Activities

1. **Dogs:**

   Therapy dogs can teach responsibility, empathy, and communication.

   Example: A child might learn to give commands like "fetch" or "stay," helping them build confidence and social skills.

2. **Horses (Equine-Assisted Therapy):**

   Riding and grooming horses improve coordination, balance, and emotional regulation.

   Example: A child riding a horse might feel a sense of accomplishment while developing their motor skills and building trust with the animal.

3. **Small Pets:**

   Guinea pigs or rabbits offer opportunities for gentle interactions and caregiving.

Example: Feeding a guinea pig or brushing a rabbit teaches patience and fosters responsibility.

Tips for Parents

1. **Supervise Interactions:**

Always ensure that interactions with animals are safe and supervised.

Example: Start with a calm, well-trained animal to build trust.

2. **Start Small:**

Begin with short, guided sessions to help the child feel comfortable.

Example: Let the child observe or pet the animal before moving to activities like walking or feeding.

Yoga and Autism: Finding Calm Through Movement

Emma's First Yoga Pose.

Emma, a six-year-old with autism, often had trouble calming down after school. Her therapist suggested yoga, and during her first session, she tried "child's pose." The soothing position, combined with slow breathing, seemed to work wonders. By the end of the session, Emma was visibly calmer and even giggled as she attempted a tree pose.

Yoga offers children with autism a way to self-regulate and improve their physical and emotional well-being.

How Yoga Helps

Yoga combines movement, breathing, and mindfulness to promote relaxation, improve motor coordination, and enhance focus. For children with autism, these structured routines can provide comfort and reduce sensory overload.

Benefits

1. **Improved Focus:** Yoga helps children concentrate on their movements and breathing.

   Example: Holding a pose like "warrior" encourages body awareness and patience.

2. **Emotional Regulation:** Breathing exercises reduce anxiety and encourage self-soothing.

   Example: Deep breathing helps children calm down during moments of frustration.

3. **Better Motor Skills:** Yoga strengthens muscles and improves flexibility.

   Example: Balancing in "tree pose" builds core strength and coordination.

Tips for Parents

1. **Choose Simple Poses:**

   Start with beginner-friendly poses like "butterfly" or "child's pose."

   Example: Guide your child gently and make it fun by comparing poses to animals (e.g., "Can you be a cat?").

2. **Focus on Breathing:**

    Teach deep breathing exercises to help your child manage stress.

    Example: Inhale for four counts, hold for four counts, and exhale for four counts.

3. **Make It Interactive:**

    Join your child in yoga sessions to make it a bonding activity.

    Example: Practice poses together, encouraging each other with smiles and high-fives.

Conclusion

Both animal-assisted therapy and yoga provide unique, complementary ways to support children with autism. While therapy animals create a sense of trust and emotional connection, yoga fosters calm and physical self-awareness. These approaches, combined with evidence-based treatments, offer children meaningful paths to growth and emotional well-being.

Message for Parents:

Explore therapies that resonate with your child's preferences and needs. Whether it's bonding with a therapy animal or discovering the joys of yoga, these methods can enhance your child's journey toward a balanced and happy life. Always consult professionals to create a tailored plan that integrates these practices effectively.

Chapter 21

Together, We Empower: The Journey of Love, Resilience, and Hope

As this book draws to a close, pause for a moment to reflect on the extraordinary journey you've undertaken. This journey, like so many others in the autism community, has likely been a winding road—marked by moments of doubt and fear, yet also illuminated by small victories and profound love. Each step you've taken, every effort you've made, has paved the way for a brighter future for your child. Whether you are a parent, caregiver, or a steadfast supporter, your resilience has unlocked doors of possibility and hope.

It's important to acknowledge the challenges you've faced along the way. There were likely days when the weight of uncertainty felt overwhelming—when the questions seemed endless, and the answers too elusive. But this path has also been rich with transformation. It has offered glimpses of your child's unique brilliance, revealed their untapped potential, and deepened the bond you share. It's a journey that requires courage, and you've shown it in abundance.

The Power of Knowledge: Turning Fear into Strength

Let's revisit Priya's story—a journey that mirrors the uncertain beginnings of so many parents. When Aarav was first diagnosed with autism, Priya was overcome by a tidal wave of emotions: fear, confusion, and an overwhelming sense of "What now?" She worried if she would ever truly understand Aarav's world or if she could give him the support he needed to thrive. The thought of the unknown loomed large, casting a shadow over her hopes for the future.

But instead of allowing fear to paralyze her, Priya chose to embrace the power of knowledge. She read every book she could find on autism, sought out specialists, and leaned on her community for guidance. Each step forward brought clarity, each piece of information another beam of light breaking through the fog. She discovered therapies that resonated with Aarav, learning how to communicate with him in ways that felt natural to his unique needs.

The transformation was profound. Aarav, who once expressed his frustration through tears and silence, learned to use picture cards to communicate. The simple act of handing his mother a card to say "I'm thirsty" was no small victory—it was a monumental leap. For Aarav, it was a way to express his needs without fear; for Priya, it was a moment of realization that her dedication had opened a door to connection.

Today, Aarav smiles more, and so does Priya. The confidence she once doubted she could find now fuels her every decision. Every time Aarav's eyes light up in understanding, every time he communicates his thoughts, Priya feels the fulfillment of a promise she made to herself: to never stop learning, to never stop believing in her son's potential.

Priya's story reminds us that knowledge isn't just power— it's transformative. It takes what feels insurmountable and makes it manageable. It turns fear into empowerment and lays the foundation for growth and understanding. Like Priya, every parent has the ability to turn uncertainty into strength, unlocking a brighter tomorrow not just for their child, but for their entire family.

Small Steps, Big Milestones

Every journey is made of small, steady steps that lead to transformative moments, and these milestones are often the most cherished. Think of Meera and her son Kabir, whose sensory sensitivities once made every mealtime a challenge. For years, Kabir ate only plain rice, shying away from foods with unfamiliar textures, colors, or smells. Meera didn't give up. She started with small, playful experiments—cutting fruits into fun shapes and making faces on his plate with bright, colorful options. Gradually, Kabir's curiosity grew. First, he touched a slice of mango. Then he tasted it. One day, to Meera's delight, Kabir asked for strawberries, his new favorite snack. That simple request symbolized months of persistence, love, and the triumph of patience over frustration.

Or take Arjun, a ten-year-old who struggled with motor coordination and avoided physical activities. His parents enrolled him in occupational therapy, where he practiced balance and coordination with games and exercises. Arjun's therapist encouraged him to try riding a bike, starting with a balance bike and slowly progressing. It wasn't easy—there were falls, tears, and moments of doubt. But one sunny afternoon, Arjun took his first solo ride down the street, his smile as bright as the sky. For his parents, it was more than a milestone; it was a symbol of resilience, growth, and the unyielding power of hope.

Overcoming Myths: Finding Confidence

For Sunita, the journey began with a heavy burden of guilt. Her son Aditya often struggled in noisy or crowded places, leading to public meltdowns that left her feeling judged. She feared others might think she was a "bad parent" or not disciplined enough. Then, she learned about sensory sensitivities and how they impact children with autism. The revelation was like a weight lifted off her shoulders. She realized Aditya's behavior wasn't about defiance but a reaction to overwhelming stimuli.

Armed with knowledge, Sunita found ways to help Aditya thrive. Noise-canceling headphones became their go-to tool, and family outings transformed. One day at the zoo, with his headphones securely on, Aditya not only enjoyed watching the animals but pointed excitedly at the giraffes, sharing his joy in a way Sunita hadn't seen before. Letting go of the myths surrounding autism allowed Sunita to step into her role as a confident, empowered parent, ready to embrace her son's needs with compassion and understanding.

Celebrating Individuality

Every child on the autism spectrum brings a unique lens to the world—a reminder that their differences are their strengths. Aarush, for example, finds immense joy in arranging blocks by size and color, creating intricate, symmetrical designs. His parents initially worried about his repetitive play but soon realized it was his way of exploring patterns and structure. By encouraging his interest, they opened the door to new learning opportunities in math and problem-solving.

Meanwhile, Aanya, with her fascination for constellations, spends hours gazing at the night sky, connecting stars with stories she's read. Her parents nurture her passion by visiting planetariums and gifting her books about astronomy. They've learned that celebrating her love for the cosmos not only builds her confidence but deepens their connection to her world.

Recognizing and honouring these unique interests helps bridge the gap between fear and understanding. It shows that every child, regardless of their challenges, has a light that shines brightest when nurtured with love and acceptance. These moments of celebration remind us that autism is not a limitation—it's a spectrum of possibilities, each child a constellation of potential waiting to be seen and cherished.

Hope for the Future

Neha remembers the day she first sat in a therapist's office, overwhelmed and teary-eyed. Her son Aarush, a gentle five-year-old, struggled with speech and social interactions. Simple tasks like greeting a classmate or asking for help seemed insurmountable. "Will he ever be able to express himself?" Neha often wondered. But instead of letting despair take hold, she leaned into hope and action.

Aarush's journey began with speech therapy sessions tailored to his needs. His therapist started with small steps, like encouraging him to say "hi" while pointing to flashcards. At home, Neha set up a sensory-friendly corner filled with soft cushions and calming toys, a space where Aarush could unwind after school. Slowly but surely, he began to find his voice. One day, while waiting at a bakery, Aarush surprised Neha by saying, "Chocolate cake, please." It was a simple phrase, but for Neha, it was a miracle.

Fast forward a few years, and Aarush now walks into his classroom each morning with a confident smile, greeting his peers with a cheerful "Good morning!" The boy who once sat quietly in the background now joins group activities and raises his hand to answer questions. Neha often reflects on how far they've come, knowing it was the combination of therapies, understanding his sensory needs, and unwavering emotional support that made the difference.

Autism: A Spectrum of Possibilities

Stories like Aarush's remind us that autism is not a limitation but a spectrum of abilities, each waiting to be nurtured. It's about focusing on strengths rather than weaknesses and believing in the power of growth. With patience, the right therapies, and a loving support system, breakthroughs—big and small—are always possible.

Parents often fear the unknown, but autism is not about what a child cannot do. It's about discovering what they *can* do and building on that foundation. Aarush's newfound confidence is a testament to the idea that progress isn't a straight line, but with persistence, the seemingly impossible becomes achievable.

A Message to Parents: You Are Not Alone

As you turn the final page of this book, take a deep breath and know this: you are not walking this journey alone. Across the world, millions of parents and caregivers are navigating similar challenges, celebrating small victories, and holding onto hope. Together, you form a global community that is changing perceptions, creating opportunities, and building brighter tomorrows for children with autism.

Celebrate every step forward, no matter how small. Whether it's a smile during a challenging day or a new word spoken after months of effort, these moments are proof of your child's resilience—and your own.

Autism is not a journey defined by limits but by endless possibilities. With knowledge, patience, and love, every child can shine in their unique way. As a parent or caregiver, you are a beacon of hope, lighting the path for your child and creating a world where they are not just accepted but celebrated. Together, we are crafting a future filled with understanding, compassion, and endless potential.

And remember: you are not alone. Together, we create a brighter tomorrow.

References
for further readings

1. Nair MKC, Russell P. Autism Spectrum Disorders. Noble Vision; 2020.

2. Dalwai SH, Gupta A, Mukherjee SB, Gaba D. Suspecting Autism and Care of Children with Autism: Guidelines for Parents. Indian Academy of Pediatrics; 2021.

3. Kumar RR, Saxena V, Gupta P, Kinjawadekar U, editors. Standard Treatment Guidelines 2022: Autism Spectrum Disorders. Indian Academy of Pediatrics; 2022.

4. Unni J, Dalwai S, Srivastav L, Seth S, Meenai Z, Multani KS. Autism: Understand and Empower. Indian Academy of Pediatrics; 2024.

5. Pfeiffer BA, Koenig K, Kinnealey M, Sheppard M, Henderson L. Effectiveness of sensory integration interventions in children with autism spectrum disorders: a pilot study. Am J Occup Ther. 2011;65(1):76-85. doi:10.5014/ajot.2011.09205. PMID: 21309374; PMCID: PMC3708964.

6. Ke X, Song W, Yang M, Li J, Liu W. Effectiveness of music therapy in children with autism spectrum disorder: A systematic review and meta-analysis. Front Psychiatry. 2022;13:905113. doi:10.3389/fpsyt.2022.905113.

7. Wang Y. Art therapy for individuals with autism spectrum disorder and depression: effectiveness and future directions. J Educ Humanit Soc Sci. 2023;22:168-74. doi:10.54097/ehss.v22i1.12415.

8. O'Haire M. Research on animal-assisted intervention and autism spectrum disorder, 2012-2015. Appl Dev Sci. 2017;21(3):200-216. doi:10.1080/10888691.2016.1243988. PMID: 31080343; PMCID: PMC6510492.

Acknowledgements

As I bring this book to completion, I am filled with gratitude for the many people who made this journey possible. Writing about autism—a topic so close to my heart—has been both a challenging and fulfilling experience, and I could not have done it alone.

First and foremost, I want to express my deepest thanks to my husband and my family. Your unwavering support, patience, and love have been my foundation. You stood by me through every late-night writing session, every moment of doubt, and every milestone reached. Your belief in me has been my greatest encouragement, and I am eternally grateful.

To my seniors and colleagues, thank you for your invaluable guidance and encouragement. Your wisdom and insights have not only shaped my understanding of autism but have also inspired me to take this step toward sharing knowledge with others. Your faith in my work gave me the confidence to pursue this project wholeheartedly.

To my patients and their families, thank you for trusting me to be a part of your journey. Your stories, courage, and resilience have been my greatest teachers. This book is a reflection of the countless moments we have shared—moments of progress, perseverance, and hope. I dedicate this work to you, for it is your strength that fuels my passion to make a difference.

This book is a testament to the collective efforts of all these incredible individuals. Thank you for being a part of this journey and for believing in the vision that brought it to life. Together, we are creating a brighter tomorrow.